"MARKET THE 'BLEEP' OUT OF IT..."

Getting Your Business Where You Want It To Be

by:
Roderick L. Harter

To my wonderful children, Rod and Christina, and my beloved grandson, Colin. I love you more than anything else in the world. You are all the inspiration I need to get up early every day and continue to work hard on my own entrepreneurial freedom.

Testimonials

"Rod Harter delivers quality work, on time – every time! Be prepared – you're going to get more than you bargained for."
– Mira Beck, Founder/CEO, Beck Audio Visual Services, LLC

"Rod Harter's first sales letter generated almost $60,000 in sales and surpassed my wildest expectations!"
– Susan Berkley, Founder/CEO, The Great Voice Company, Inc.

"As a business owner and fellow copywriter, I have great respect for Rod Harter's highly effective style of writing. I highly recommend his services to any small business owner or entrepreneur looking to take a quantum leap in their sales and marketing efforts."
– Chris Hurn, Founder/CEO, Fountainhead Commercial Capital

"Great copywriters are proven because consumers vote with their money. That's why people like Rod Harter are so rare and so valuable. If you enter the marketing jungle in search of riches, just be sure you walk with this man at your side."
– Brian L. Fricke, CFP® Financial Management Concepts; Fee Only® Financial Planner, author, speaker, & Incredible Retirement® Expert

"As a tax strategist, my niche market is the affluent, representing the top 1% of taxpayers. It's important our marketing message be clearly stated whenever we communicate with our customers. Rod's delivery is always on the mark."
– Bob J. Baker, CEO, Asset Strategist, Inc.

"Rod Harter has done an outstanding job for us on several of our marketing campaigns. He knows all the emotional 'purchase triggers' and buy buttons that make Rod's copywriting style so valuable to a business owner."
– Danny Peterson, Owner & Founder, Integrity Home Pro
–

"When I need help with really good direct-response style copy, I always look to Rod Harter – he's my number one go-to guy! Rod's work is wonderful. Use him and you'll be recommending his services to everyone you know… just as we do!"
– Diane Conklin, President/Founder, *Complete Marketing Systems*, author, coach, event planner, and speaker

"My company, BGI Systems, hosts two big insurance events per year. We hired Rod Harter several years ago after experiencing disappointing results with our two previous copywriters. Rod's done an outstanding job for us. He always meets our critical goals and deadlines and keeps us well informed throughout the writing process."
– Bill Gough, President/CEO BGI Systems, author, speaker, and entrepreneur

"Rod Harter is not only good – he's creative and has a keen sense of what it takes to write effective direct response marketing campaigns. There are no trophies in business for being close. You either hit your mark, or starve. Use Rod once, and you won't work with anyone else."
– Nigel Worrall, freelance photographer, video, author, production, and editor at *Florida Leisure*

"As a published author, hiring a copywriter to write on my behalf was a bit uncomfortable, to say the least. Yet Rod's quick turnaround, writing style, and content 'blew me away.' He quickly put my fears at ease. Trust Rod's experience. Let him do what he does best: Drive business to your door through thought-provoking, information grabbing, content-rich marketing campaigns."
– Traci Bild, CEO & President, Bild & Company, Integrated Healthcare Solutions, author, speaker, and entrepreneur

"Rod Harter knows how to write great direct-response campaigns with all the emotional 'purchase triggers'. He's been a breath of fresh air for us. He's a perfect match if you're really serious about your marketing and committed to growing your business. Rod WILL make your phone ring!"
– Scott Young, Owner, Advanced Home Technologies

"In business, the success formula is simple. You either stand out or risk being lumped in with everyone else. Ordinary businesses get ordinary results. Rod Harter is no 'ordinary' copywriter. He's extremely talented. He delivers incredible copy that always pleases both my staff and our clients."
– Nick Nanton, Esq., Cofounder, The Dicks + Nanton Celebrity Branding Agency, speaker, author, and entrepreneur

"Rod and his company, Specialty Marketing Consulting, have done wonders for my business. Their service and quality of work have exceeded my wildest expectations. Rod's brilliant, 'outside-the-box', marketing strategies have been amazing. I no longer feel like I'm working alone in an isolation chamber. What a breath of fresh air."
– Veronica Edwards, Broker & Owner, Elite Real Estate & Property Management, author, speaker, and consultant

"Rod Harter is a master at his craft! He's a great direct-response copywriter. We hired him to write a marketing campaign to our cell phone retail agents. The campaign was a huge success."
– Nile Nickel, President, Revenue Assurance Holdings, Inc.

"Rod Harter is a tremendous resource to have in your computer or Rolodex. Don't lose his number. We recently hired Rod to write a couple of marketing campaigns for us. He did an outstanding job on both projects. I admire Rod's ability to create that 'must have now' factor in everything he writes."
– Dr. Johnathon Berns, FifeSource Family Chiropractic

"Rod Harter is a man amongst boys. He's done wonders for my business. I cannot thank him enough for all he has done."
– Howard Ingham, Owner, Premiere Pulmonary Services

"If you're really serious about taking your business to the next level, I cannot recommend Rod Harter's copywriting talents enough. Rod is a top notch direct response marketer and copywriter.

He's knowledgeable, focused, and results-driven. Most importantly, when taking on a copywriting project, he works with you as a consultant, really getting to the nitty-gritty of defining and understanding your prospective client, working to figure out what their 'hot button' might be, and getting them to respond and 'raise their hand'. If you don't get a response in your direct mail piece, it just doesn't matter, and Rod is all about getting a response!!! Of the many marketing, consulting and copywriting experts out there who I pay attention to, Rod is – without a doubt – one of my favorites. I am proud to have him on my team as my 'go-to' copywriter!!"
– Larry Weinstein, CPA, Tax Solution Specialist, author, speaker, and consultant

"Rod Harter stands out because he gets results. Struggling entrepreneurs and business owners should give him a call. Rod always provides great ideas every time I consult with him. I believe people will be impressed with what he can do for their businesses."
– Jeffrey R. Prager, D.D.S., *Bellingham Smile and Sleep Center*

"Hiring Rod is like having a trusted guide for your adventure... an adventure that leads to profits. When I first heard that direct-response copywriting is the foundation of any business message, I thought what many people probably think: It has to look 'professional'. What I discovered through working with Rod is, it can look professional AND have a lot of personality and still perform like a world-class salesperson. In a world where anyone can claim to be a copywriter, Rod's results speak for themselves."
– Jordan Salamone, Owner, MerchantAccountTampa.com

Your Key To Marketing Success
By John B. Kelly

Today, my insurance company is an in-demand resource for individuals and progressive businesses alike. My client list includes some of the most respected and successful names in Central Florida. Several companies you would undoubtedly recognize.

Much of our success has come from the unique way we interact with our clients. We give them something they've never found anywhere else – professional integrity delivered with a special, human touch. Much of how we communicate with our clients is through our marketing.

The key for me occurred several years ago when my eyes were opened to a form of marketing that allows us to communicate with our clients with professionalism and personality. Our monthly, front-porch style newsletter is a perfect example of how we've furthered our relationships with our valued clients.

Our big breakthrough marketing-wise came from my introduction to direct response marketing, thanks to my father-in-law, Rod Harter. For almost 20 years, he's been working side-by-side with the giants in the direct marketing industry. His podcast, ***Marketing You Can Do Right Now***, is a routine part of my daily commute. I also enjoy reading his ***"On-Target Marketing"*** newsletter, cover-to-cover, every month.

It's hard to put into words just how much the strategies of direct response marketing have influenced our business. It's also hard to convey exactly how incredibly valuable this

book is that you have in your hands. These strategies will be a game changer for you and your business.

I know plenty of wealthy business owners who'll treasure the information in this book and keep it close by for quick access to the cutting-edge strategies here.

There isn't a business owner or entrepreneur out there that won't benefit enormously from what's in these pages. I don't care *how* obscure your service is or how "different" you think your business is.

You can make excuses, or you can make money. You can't do both. All I can say now is… dive in and take action. You'll soon see what all the fuss is about.

You're in for a treat.

John B. Kelly
Partner – Co-Founder
Financial Centers Of America

John B. Kelly is a partner and co-founder of *Financial Centers of America Financial Centers* is an independent insurance and retirement agency located in historic Winter Park, Florida. Since its inception in 2001, John and the company have supported several company-leading agents in the industry while also being recognized for exceptional personal production.

Learn more about our services by visiting our website –
www.fcoaonline.com
Or contact me directly –
Office: (407) 679-1599 Email: johnb@fcoaonline.com

Introduction

This is not just a book of good ideas. This is a book of timeless small business marketing strategies used by successful business owners and entrepreneurs all over the world. These marketing principles have helped me, and hundreds of my clients all over the country, live and enjoy extraordinary businesses.

Keep this book handy. My hope is that you'll read it several times and keep it on the corner of your desk, dog-eared and beaten up. Write on it. Highlight the areas most important to you. Use it as a reference guide until you know these techniques backwards and forwards.

The marketing strategies in this book are not new. They've been with us for almost a century. Marketing has been around for quite some time. There have been hundreds of books written, courses taken, video products produced, and countless seminars attended. They all have one thing in common. They "sold" you the book. You "purchased" the videos. You "signed" up for the seminar. **They got you to purchase their product or service.**

They marketed you.

Anything and everything can be marketed. Whether you're the new dentist in the neighborhood or the best gasket setter in the county, marketing your goods or services must be an essential part of your business plan. It must also find a place in your budget.

But *how* should you be marketing? If you're like most small businesses or independent professionals, you're probably doing one of two things. You're copying what your competitors are doing, or you're advertising like the "Big Boys" do. Why wouldn't you? After all, "It works for them; it has to work for me." Right?

WRONG.

Let's say you opened a new dry cleaning service in your city and you need business. What do you do? If you're like most business owners, you look around at what your competitors are doing and copy them. The trouble with this idea is nobody knows what the best, most cost-effective strategy to market their business is.

Or, you may have done what I did when I started my business 17 years ago. I tried to market it like Coke, IBM, and GM. The problem with that approach is the big boys spend millions of dollars on marketing and advertising, which I didn't have.

There's a much better option.

It's called "Direct Response Marketing", and as you read this book, it is going to open your eyes to a completely new world of opportunities to grow your business much faster than you ever thought possible.

Direct response marketing isn't new. In fact, it's been around since the early 1920s. It's a unique and different way to market and advertise your business that will <u>set you apart from your competition</u>. It has many facets. It allows you to develop marketing and advertising that is fine-tuned and laser focused to your target audiences.

I use three pillars for success at my company: **attract 'em, convert 'em, and keep 'em.**

By using direct response marketing, we help our clients *attract* new business, *convert* customers and clients to use their product or services, while increasing their customer base, and *keep* their existing clients over the long haul. In a way, we help them create their own "Direct Response Profit Lab".

The following chapters contain all the ingredients you need to get started.

Table of Contents

CHAPTER 1

In The Beginning

As a kid, I remember my dad always telling me, "Son, whatever you end up doing with your life, make damn sure you find your way to marketing." All those years ago, and I can still hear my father's deep voice repeating those penetrating words.

It's interesting how things turned out.

I come from a family in aviation. My dad worked for Pan American World Airways for more than 40 years. His success had a big influence on my career path. As an impressionable teenager, I'd become spoiled with our ability to travel around the world, usually in first class. It was something I'd become accustomed to doing. I was never able to part ways with my love of aviation and the excitement of traveling all over the world. As a result, I decided to follow my dreams.

On September 1, 1973 in Miami, Delta Air Lines hired me. It was a great career choice involving almost 25 years of sales, marketing, and advertising. Looking back, I wouldn't have changed a thing.

Throughout my tenure with Delta, I received outstanding training in advertising and marketing, and not just for the airline industry. I received the kind of experience revered by many large companies. A marketing representative from Delta could walk down the street with head held high knowing he'd been properly trained in many areas of marketing.

Yet, with all the marketing and advertising I learned at Delta, there was still something missing, and it was a big item.

Our advertising didn't have that personable, 'human touch'. Instead, we spent millions of dollars every month promoting our brand. All that money Delta spent on advertising, and still something very important was lacking.

Personality.

Delta couldn't advertise like a small business. For that matter, no big company can do that. Instead, Delta had to focus on what they did best, which was fly millions of people safely around the world. When it came to advertising, we did what every other big business does. We threw a huge net over a huge global audience, hoping to snag our share of the market.

My career was great, but as they say, nothing lasts forever. One day on my way to work, something hit me. I suddenly realized I'd had enough. The airline industry had changed to the point where I was no longer having fun. Rather than spending another 10-15 years doing something I wasn't enjoying, I decided to retire.

I went to work for a small mortgage company. The best part of working in the mortgage industry was it allowed me to work with my daughter, Christina, for a few years. Christina was going to school at The University of Central Florida. She was looking for part-time work. My company hired her, and we ended up being a team together. I was a loan officer, and Christina was a processor. They were great times… some of the best years of my life. There was just one exception. I wasn't bringing enough new clients in the door. I was getting by but not like I wanted. I tried marketing my business to realtors and financial planners. I mailed hundreds of 'corporate-style' letters to them, over and over. Unfortunately, nothing seemed to work, until one day, a financial planner received one of my letters. He gave me a call and invited me to his office for a meeting.

The gentleman's name was Brian Fricke. We spent a little time getting to know each other. About the time we were wrapping things up, he asked me if I'd heard of something called "direct response" marketing. I told him I wasn't familiar with it. He suggested I check it out. He said it had done wonders for his business.

As I walked to my car after my meeting with Brian, I thought, what a great guy. But in all fairness to him, he had no idea what my background was. He didn't know I had almost 25 years of advertising and marketing experience under my belt with a Fortune 500 company. From my perspective, I damn sure didn't need a small business owner giving me advice about how I should market my business. It wasn't long before I found out otherwise.

About six months later, Brian invited me back to his office to discuss a client of his. At the end of our conversation, he asked me again if I'd had a chance to research direct response marketing. My answer was the same – no. However, this time, I was far more interested in what he had to say. You see, earlier that month, I had mailed about 200 letters to a targeted list of prospective clients. I didn't get one response… not one! This time Brian had my full and undivided attention. It turned out to be some of the best advice I ever received.

Over the next few years, I began writing lead generation copy. Not the kind of worthless leads sold on the Internet that aren't worth the paper they're printed on. These were *real* leads. It was a different form of marketing. I began attracting the kind of prospects I wanted to do business with. Instead of chasing people, they were coming to me.

Brian's recommendation came more than 17 years ago. Since then, I've read hundreds of books on the subject of direct response marketing. I've also attended dozens of seminars and conferences all over the country. I have forged many wonderful relationships with business owners who've built their businesses on the foundation of direct response marketing.

I just happened to be in the right place at the right time. Brian and I met at a pivotal point in my life. With his help, I discovered a much smarter way to market my business by being far more personable and friendly.

Direct response marketing transformed my business. It worked for me – and it will work for you. It doesn't matter if you're a plumber, dentist, doctor, candle maker, care center, or anything else. Once you understand the basic fundamentals, everything will begin to make sense. You'll discover, as I discovered, it's not about "what" you're marketing – it's about "how" you market it.

My hope is that the pages within this book will open your eyes to a radically new and different way to market and grow your business. I hope you're ready because something very special awaits you. All I ask is that you keep an open mind until you've read the entire book and understand the concept.

You may be thinking to yourself, "Rod, I hate having to learn something new." Believe me, it's worth it.

I too was hesitant. At my age, the last thing I wanted to do was learn a new way to promote and market my business. I was very sure I knew what I was doing. As it turned out, I was wrong. Brian's advice changed my business – and my life.

Allow me to explain my point by telling a short, childhood story. I was raised in Miami. One day when I was about 12 years old, my dad decided it was time for me to learn how to skin dive. We packed up our car and drove to the local marina. We got on our boat and headed east, about 3-4 miles off shore. When we reached the spot, my dad threw anchor. Then, in his deep, authoritative voice he said, "Put on your mask and fins Son, and jump in." I couldn't believe what he was asking me to do. After all, we were out in the middle of the ocean in very deep water. I couldn't even see land.

After thinking about it for several minutes, I finally put on my gear and eased into the deep blue water. I hung on the ladder a few minutes until I could catch my breath and conjure up enough courage to put my face below the surface. That moment was all I needed.

In a flash, all my fear and anxiety disappeared, replaced by a huge adrenalin rush. The water was crystal clear. Hundreds of beautiful tropical fish were swimming around huge coral formations. I'd never seen anything so beautiful in all my life. To this day, that moment remains one of the greatest experiences of my life. And when I stop and reflect on it, that moment would have never happened had my father not forced me to leave my comfort zone. My dad opened my eyes to something that changed my life forever.

It was a lesson I'll never forget.

I was also sure I didn't need the marketing advice Brian Fricke gave me almost 18 years ago. In both instances, I was absolutely sure whatever advice they were trying to give me, I didn't need.

So, what's the moral of my story? Well, sometimes, when you *think* you "know"…you don't.

Far too often we make decisions without knowing all the facts. It's human nature and part of our DNA. Oftentimes, "What we're not up on, we're down on." My hope is that you'll keep an open mind about direct response marketing *until* you've read this entire book.

I'm sure you'll agree. You don't know what you're missing until you dive in!

Are you ready?

Okay. Take a big breath.

Together, we're about to take a deep dive into the exciting world of direct response marketing.

CHAPTER 2
Marketing – Your Best Employee

If you're like me, you hate sad news. When it comes to marketing, one of the saddest things I hear is when a business owner tells me, "I don't have time to market my business."

It hurts my ears when I hear that. That's like saying, "I just bought a great new car, but I don't have time to get to the gas station." We all know a car can't run without gas. Your business is no different. It cannot run and grow quickly and successfully without marketing.

Marketing is the fuel that runs your business. It can't run at its full potential without the right fuel that comes in the form of marketing and advertising.

Look around at any highly successful local, regional, or national level business in your niche, and you'll find that marketing is a core part of their success.

I'm not asking you to suddenly change everything you're doing to advertise and market your business – not *yet* anyway. All I'm asking you to do at this point is refrain from disbelieving what I'm sharing with you until you've seen all the information I'm going to share with you in this book.

These are tested and proven strategies used by top marketers all over the world for more than a century. Direct response marketing works well for millions of businesses in every niche, business, and industry under the sun including:

• Sales careers

- Business to business and industrial industries
- Retail sales
- Professional practices
- Service businesses
- Restaurants
- And most importantly… E-commerce and online businesses

I hear stories all the time from business owners who've had huge breakthroughs from implementing the same marketing strategies we're going to cover in this book.

"But, MY Business Is Different"

I'd like to have a dime every time I've had a business owner say to me, "Rod, this is great stuff, but my business is different."

With all due respect, your business is NOT different, but even if it is, direct response marketing still works. When you do it right, it will have a dramatic impact on your bottom line even if your business is unique.

These comments, however, usually come from struggling business owners who, in their heart, believe they have a better mousetrap. You never hear those comments from any business owners who have taken the time to implement the marketing systems discussed in this book. It typically comes from people who are close-minded.

Unfortunately many business owners have this idea that their business should be run a certain way. They're not open to new and different ideas. Or maybe they're scared to make a change. If you have this phobia, try looking at your marketing as "individual pieces" or "campaigns". If you break it down into manageable pieces, it won't be such a daunting task.

Always remember, you're not your client. Always live in *their* world. Think like them, not like you.

The "big boys" play a different game. They have millions of dollars to spend on advertising. They can afford to invest huge sums of money on TV, radio, stadium signage, and flying blimps over sporting events. You and I can't afford to do that. As small business owners, our rules for advertising and marketing are much simpler.

Every dollar you spend on marketing today must be carefully tracked and measured and put back in your till as soon as possible. Trying to copy the big, brand name companies is a quick recipe for disaster. It's like a rabbit behaving like a lion. You'll soon be eaten alive.

Most small businesses rely on location, word of mouth, and repeat business. Some may do an occasional ad campaign, but sparsely and with no consistency. They may send out an occasional letter or postcard. When they don't get a good response, they lose faith in marketing and give up. Direct response marketing requires much more consistency and perseverance. It's not something you can just do once in a while or when business is slow.

You must look at your marketing budget the same way you look at salaries. You wouldn't think twice about missing a payday for your employees, would you? Of course not. It's time to start thinking about your business as one of your employees, and your marketing and advertising budget as your business's salary. After all, you work hard to make sure your business is the best it can be.

Setting a budget is the *only* way you can start and maintain marketing and advertising. You must look at it as an ongoing, necessary investment in your business. This is an absolute in order for your business to survive and grow over the long haul.

Point being, whether you're spending millions a month or hundreds a month, you've got to commit to your marketing and advertising efforts. It's the only way your business can grow quickly and profitably. If you're unwilling to dedicate a portion of your business's revenue on marketing and advertising on a consistent basis, then you've also just found yourself some free time because there's no need for you to read any further. You will find your business stuck in a rut and unable to grow further.

My hope is you picked this book up for one of several reasons. Either you want to make a change in the direction your business is going, or you're curious about *this* form of marketing. Whatever your reason, you're about to have your eyes opened to a radically different way to grow your business. And once you start using it, your business will begin to rise, head and shoulders above your competition.

If things are going "okay" and business is brisk but you want to do better, this book will help you do that.

If you're struggling, there are simple, easy-to-follow strategies here that will have an immediate and profound impact on your business, even in a tough economy with stiff competition from low-priced competitors.

Pay Yourself First

Treat your business like a personal IRA account. Just as a financial planner would tell you to pay yourself first, you MUST do the same for your business.

You might be thinking to yourself, "I don't have the extra money in my budget to pay myself first." <u>You MUST find it</u>. Do a careful review of your expenses. Consult with your accountant. Do whatever is necessary to pay your business first.

So what's a good amount to set aside for your marketing

budget? A good starting place is 5% of your business's gross annual income. Instead of a fixed dollar amount, use a percentage. This is to your advantage. No matter what your company's gross annual income is, the percentage will remain constant.

For example, if your company grossed $300,000 last year, then you should have budgeted $15,000 for your marketing and advertising. If you grossed $5M, then you should have allocated $250,000. You get the picture. The secret is, come hell or high water, hook or crook, your advertising and marketing budget must be a fixed part of your business.

Let's use the $300,000 as an example. If you grossed $300k last year, that gives you $15,000 this year to spend on marketing and advertising. Use it wisely. Does your business call for daily, weekly, or monthly advertising? Is your market seasonal and allow you to advertise during certain parts of the year?

If you want to use your budget on a monthly basis, then simply divide the $15,000 into 12 parts. That gives you $1,250 per month to run your ads, put together promotions, and mail a printed, monthly newsletter. This kind of consistent marketing will get your business's name out to the purchasing public.

Remember what I said earlier. You work like a junkyard dog at making your business a success. Treat it like you would your number one employee.

Keep your business happy. Pay it well. Pay it consistently.

CHAPTER 3
What *Is* Direct Response Marketing?

For thousands of marketers around the world, direct response marketing is the ONLY way to go. In their eyes, it's the goose that laid the golden egg. Others refer to direct marketing as *"The Eighth Wonder Of The World"* because it works like crazy!

According to the Direct Selling Association, over 18 million people were involved in direct response marketing in the United States in 2014 with estimated retail sales reaching $34.5 billion, a 5.5% increase from 2013. The direct marketing industry continues to see steady growth. Many small business owners generated more revenue in 2014 than any year previously.

Almost 35 billion dollars was generated by direct marketing in 2014. As you can see, direct marketing isn't going anywhere.

Throughout this book, you'll hear me refer to it as "direct response" marketing or "direct marketing". They're essentially one in the same.

Direct marketing occurs when businesses contact their prospects, customers, and clients through a multitude of channels. It may include sending mail, e-mails, talking on the phone, and/or meeting in person. Direct marketing messages involve a specific "call to action," such as "Call this toll-free number" or "Click this link to subscribe." The results of such campaigns are immediately measurable, as a business can track how many customers have responded through a message's call to action.

In contrast, general advertising – for example, a billboard promoting a brand concept or product awareness – while seen by the customer, does not call for a specific response and therefore cannot be easily measured. A marketer doesn't know exactly how effective such a billboard is or how many people are thinking about and buying the product because of the billboard. However, because of the specific call to action in direct response marketing, he or she does know exactly how many people responded to a direct mailing or email.

CHAPTER 4
The Sales Letter

It's hard to beat the numerous benefits of a great sales letter. If you stop and think about it, the ability to zero in on your ideal prospect makes a direct response marketing sales letter incredibly powerful. No other form of marketing comes close because it allows you to be very specific and target your ideal audience.

Can you think of any other type of marketing besides the sales letter that's so affordable and gives you as much flexibility? I sure can't.

A great sales letter is like having a superstar salesperson working for your company on the street, knocking on doors, building relationships, and closing deals around the clock, 7 days a week.

Imagine that.

Can you match that level of marketing any other way? No way. Not even close.

A good sales letter puts you in control. It tells your prospect how you want them to respond. You can send them to your website, a landing page, or a 24-hour free recorded message.

Let's dive into this a bit deeper and look at some of the specifics of a great sales letter. But first…

Let Me Ease Your Mind

If you're like many business owners we consult with, you may already understand the effectiveness of a good sales letter but don't have the confidence to write one yourself.

I'm here to tell you… <u>YOU CAN</u>!

You don't have to be the next Stephen King or John Grisham. You don't have to know how to write a bestselling novel. You're simply transferring the same things you'd say to a prospect standing in front of you, onto paper.

You're a good salesperson… right? Of course you are. Otherwise you wouldn't own your own business. Nobody understands your business better than you. Nobody knows your products and services more than you. Nobody knows what makes your business better than your competitors.

A word of caution here – when most people write a sales letter, they focus on the wrong things. They think too much about having perfect grammar or writing to a large group of people. They try to make their letter have the look and feel of a corporate-style letter.

You don't want that.

You want the opposite of a rigid, formal letter. There's certainly nothing wrong with having a great command of the English language, but formal English is NOT what makes a great sales letter work. Your reader wants to feel your "personality", like you were talking to them in their home or having a beer together. That's how you bond with people. It's just you, talking to one person. Once you understand how to do this, you'll attract more buyers and close more deals.

You already have the resources in you. You just have to pull them out and get them on paper. With my guidance, we're going to arrange your words in a way that's easy for your prospect to read. By the time you finish this chapter, you're going to know how to do that. You'll be able to make your business stand out and be different, which will bring you more sales.

How Long Should Your Letter Be?

Many business owners think that a sales letter should be brief, that people won't read a long sales letter. That's not completely true. There is a time and a place for a short sales letter of course. For the most part however, you never want to cut yourself short.

Would you ever tell your best superstar salesperson to only say a few words to a prospect? Would you even confine them to any certain number of words? Of course you wouldn't.

That would be unthinkable.

The only people who are going to read your sales letter are the ones who find your subject interesting. However, if your letter is vague or boring, or if you've sent it to the wrong audience, it won't be read. It won't matter how long or short your letter is. It won't be read.

People won't read sales letters for fun or entertainment. They will read your letter because it provides valuable, helpful information they NEED to know. Years of testing have shown that people will read a long sales letter if your subject appeals to them. They'll read it regardless of how long or short it is. Always think of your reader as a "prospect" standing before you, seeking information from you.

Your goal is straightforward. Give your prospect enough information so they can make an informed decision and take action.

Finding Your Starving Crowd

Legendary direct marketer Gary Halbert would often ask his students, "If you and I both owned a hamburger stand, and we were in a contest together to see who could sell the most hamburgers... what advantages would you like to have on your side to help you win?"

Most people would say they wanted "superior meat" or the "best location," or "lowest prices". Halbert would tell them they could have all those advantages and more, and he'd still beat the pants off them. The most important advantage, Halbert explained, is to make sure you have a "starving crowd"!

Think about it... if you get your product or service in front of the right audience, your "starving crowd", you can't lose. It doesn't matter if you're the new guy in town or competing against the big box companies. You're going to win.

A rabid audience that "needs" what you're putting in front of them will respond to a letter.

Know Your Prospect

Know as much about your prospect as you can. By that, I mean you should think like your prospect.

After a long day on the ocean, a small group of fishermen gathered in the local pub to enjoy a beer together. The fishermen were in the middle of a bad slump. Nobody was catching any fish, except for one guy. One of his fishing buddies asked the old man, the one catching all the fish, what his secret was. The bearded, weather-beaten fisherman cleared his throat, and quietly said, "Gentlemen, my secret is simple. You guys think like fishermen. I think like the fish."

From now on, think like your prospects. Live in *their* world, not yours. Stop guessing what you think they'd like, or what you think they'd be interested in buying from you.

Climb into their heads. Enter the conversation already going on in your prospect's mind. Give this strategy some deep thought. Ask yourself:

- What is your prospect constantly thinking about?
- What's keeping your prospect up at night?
- What are they secretly mad at?
- What do they *really* want to achieve?
- What do they keep dreaming about?

Before you start writing, determine what's most important to your prospect. What problem are you going to solve for them?

Send your letter to a specific, targeted audience. Cast a much smaller net, to a finely tuned market. The key is not just writing a good letter, but mailing it to the right audience using the right medium. This kind of marketing is a fraction of the cost of traditional advertising, but will produce much greater results.

Let me say it again… right audience, right offer, right medium. You can't just have two out of three components of the formula right. All three factors carry equal importance. Failure to do this, and you won't get a good response, no matter who writes your letter.

The Direct Marketing Sales Letter Formula

There are many direct response formulas. One of the more popular ones is called AIDA: Attention, Interest, Desire, Action.

Job #1: Get your reader's attention. Without their attention, you have nothing.

Job #2: Hold your reader's attention. This is done by creating interest or curiosity by making your reader want to know more. Copywriters refer to this process as "the slippery slope." You gently guide your reader through your letter by making it easy for them to read.

Job #3: Have a clear reason for them to respond now – a "call to action." You must provide clear instructions as to what you want your reader to do, how you want them to respond.

People will follow directions if you're clear about what you want them to do. Make it easy for them to understand.

The Hook

Okay, let's start with the hook, your attention-getter.

You must have a great hook, or to use a more common term, a headline. This is your grabber. Newspapers have been doing it for centuries. When you pick up a newspaper, what's the first thing you see? The grabber. The hook. The thing that makes you read further. Without it, it's like having the world's best engine in the world's fastest car, but you forgot to install the starter.

Famous ad man, David Ogilvy, said, "On average, five times as many people read the headline as read the body copy. When you have written your headline, you've spent eighty cents out of your dollar."

You can write the best, content-rich copy the world has ever seen, but without the proper set up, no one will ever see it. That's just human nature. We're like that game fish. We become fixed on that shiny, silver lure. We want to be enticed. We want to be led. So give them what they want! Be sure you have their attention. Without it, you'll lose them.

The headline includes any combination of pre-head, main headline and/or subheads. This is where you instantly grab your reader's attention, make your announcement, and tell your reader what's in it for them in an exciting way. This area is also known as the "deck" copy.

Next are the opening words, also known as the "lead" or "introduction". This is where you build more emotion. Depending on your market and hook, this could be any of the major emotions… such as anger, guilt, fear, pride, etc.

The Body Copy

The body of your sales letter must be content rich. By that I mean you've spent all that energy on making sure you have the right hook. Make sure you don't let them down with dull, boring information. Nothing will lose your reader faster.

Don't bore your reader with junk or filler. You only have their attention for a few moments. Take full advantage of it. People aren't going to spend much time reading something that doesn't hold their attention. Even the best hook in the world won't hold *anyone*, unless you keep their interest.

The body of a good sales letter has many features. It must have personality – you're personality. People like dealing with another person. Chapter 5 will cover this subject in detail. We'll discuss ways to tap into your personality and how to put it into words.

Turn the features of your business into benefits for your prospect. This may sound difficult, but it's one of the easiest things to do and has some of the best return on investment (ROI) you can ask for.

A quick example might be, instead of writing as a business feature, "We're open 24 hours a day," write it from your prospect's point of view as a benefit. "Come shop when it's convenient for you. We're open 24 hours a day." See how you've turned your feature into their benefit? Chapter 8 covers this amazing marketing tool in detail.

After this, comes the "close".

The Close

You can do many things here, including injecting a little scarcity into the offer. Have your reader think about the consequences of NOT taking action. Remind them of the benefits/value/guarantee/scarcity, etc.

Always include a sense of finality. It helps if your sales letter has a "valid till" notion to it. It can be an expiration date, "offer good through," or "now is the time to act." You know this to be true. How many times do you see an ad for something you really want, or need, and it says "valid through Friday only"?

Most of us carry that fear of not wanting to push anyone away by being too pushy. Bury that worry.

Most people want to be sold. As smart as the average consumer may be, they want your help. They want that nudge to make the decision and close the deal. Don't go hitting them over the head with a bat, though. There are subtle ways to help them make up their minds. *Now* is the best time to persuade them.

The P.S.

As you close out your letter, don't forget the P.S. You know what happens when you receive a letter with a P.S. at the end of it, of course. You read it every time because it sparks that same "interest gene" that your headline sparked. People are curious, and this is a great place to recap your offer. Basically, tell 'em what you're going to tell 'em, tell 'em, and then tell 'em what you just told 'em.

Dual Path Readership

When your prospects receive your sales letter, they will typically fall into one of three categories as a reader:

Skimmers – These people will skim a page up and down quickly to get a quick overview of what you're selling. They're usually quick to act and likely have their minds already made up before they even get to the end of the page.

Jumpers – These people spend more time on the page than skimmers but less than bookworms. They'll skim the page, but then if something catches their attention – they'll jump into the copy and read it thoroughly.

Bookworms – These people will read everything, top to bottom… every single word. They're typically slower decision makers and tend to think things over. They'll want every single ounce of detail before making a decision. Or sometimes, they just like to read.

True readers will read most of what you write. These people are great, but they're rare. Most people will first skim through your letter. They'll breeze over your copy, stopping to read only what grabs their attention.

Smart marketers address all three types of readers by using something called "dual path readership". It takes into account both the true reader and the skimmer. Simply break your copy up into short, easy-to-read paragraphs. The easier your copy is to read, the better your response will be. Read through your copy and highlight the most important sentence in each paragraph. Next, separate the highlighted sentences and turn them into subheads. Duel path readership allows you to "sell" the person who is skimming through your copy. Headlines and subheads separate busy copy so it's "easy" on the eyes. It makes it easier for your reader to make a buying decision. Refer to the examples on pages 129 and 130 to see how I break up paragraphs into easy-to-read subheads.

A Great Sales Letter Has A Long Shelf Life

Another great feature of a well-written sales letter is it has no expiration date. Once you've written it, you can use it again and again. It may take a bit of editing, but you can shape and mold the same letter to fit almost any campaign.

Pretty exciting stuff, isn't it. But before you run out and become the next "sales letter guru", keep this in mind. The sales letter is not a "one time event". Similar to your marketing and advertising budget, the sales letter is something that requires follow up – lots of follow up. Persistence pays. In fact, Chapter 10 is titled "Turn Persistence Into Pay Dirt."

CHAPTER 5
How To Write With Personality

Personality. Aaaaah yes… where would we be without one? Some say you'd be as dull as a bag of hammers if you had no personality.

It's time to look at your business the same way.

You know what I mean, right? You've been on plenty of websites or read articles that read like a phone book. They're dry and bland, with about as much personality as a log. It's as though the person writing the copy went out of their way to suck the life right out of you.

When you write better copy, specifically with more personality, it will help you:

- Drive more traffic to your website.
- Increase opt-ins on your squeeze page.
- Get more of your emails opened, and generate higher response from those who open and read your emails.
- Convert more readers into actual buyers when they read your sales letters.
- Fuel your ability to make ongoing, long-term sales and profits.

All of which makes you MUCH MORE MONEY!

Tap Into The Power Of Your Personality

Oh the times, they are a changin'!

Never at any point in history has there been as many ways for consumers to get their information. It's very crowded out there. In order for you to compete, and get noticed, you have to stand out.

That separation in your marketplace starts with who you are – your personality. Your words set the tone for how you come across to your reader.

The fastest way for you to attract people is based on the way you connect with them, the way you express yourself, and the way you come across to your audience.

Writing with personality is not about making sure you have perfect grammar or keeping a certain level of business formality. In fact, most of the time, it's exactly the opposite.

The big culprit of copy that gets no response is usually a lack of personality. For some reason, people often sequester their personality when they write. They almost make a conscious effort to hide it. Often they don't even realize they're doing it, or they think it would be unprofessional to let it show.

Showing your personality is like the difference between color and black and white TV. When you turn up the knob on your personality, it's like turning the dial from B & W to vivid color. When you let your personality come through, you shine. You become vibrant and alive. Your personality takes center stage and you become "human" to your prospects and clients instead of just another impersonal company.

In order to get engagement from your reader, you've got to "pump a little life" into your copy. Make it breathe.

Real, live, human beings are reading your letters, postcards, websites, and emails. Give them a reason to want to read on. Asking your reader to stay connected with you as they slog through stale and uninspiring copy is asking too much of them. Without that personal, emotional connection, you'll be up a creek without a paddle.

Buying decisions are made from emotion. Logic eventually kicks in, but for the vast majority of consumers, emotion is what creates trust and makes sales happen.

The idea that emotion influences the decisions we make is nothing new. Emotion, and its role in direct marketing, has been tested and studied extensively for more than a century.

When you give your business a "personality", you immediately open the door and say, "Come on in. This is who I am."

The fact is, people like doing business with other people. They want to work with a person who is honest and open and trustworthy.

When you sit down and write a sales letter, do your fingers lock up? If so, you're not alone. It happens to most people when they try to write. They talk one way and write another. When they write, their personality suffers.

But this is an enormous opportunity for you to stand out because most of today's advertising and marketing stinks. The majority of it is stale and one-dimensional. Your reader doesn't want that. They want YOU. They want to "feel" your personality and connect with a real person because there's so little of that out there. So how can you get that personality on paper?

Informal Conversation Is The Single Best Way To Make Your Writing More Personal

If you look at the hottest, most successful small business marketers, you'll find that when it comes to marketing their products and services, they've learned how to talk to their audience using everyday words and clichés like *stacking the deck, lightening fast, have your cake and eat it too, taken to the cleaners, a king's ransom, like money in the bank, worth its weight in gold,* etc. They're the same colloquial phrases we use to talk to people we know.

The next time you talk to a close friend or anybody in an informal setting, notice how often you hear expressions like *easier said than done, no time flat, long shot,* and so on. You're almost guaranteed to hear at least one of these phrases in every informal conversation. Often you'll hear many more than that.

Obviously there's more to informal conversation than just using idioms, but the point is to write like you speak in an informal setting. Have fun and be sincere. Show enthusiasm for what you're saying and stay positive.

Of course, you also need to think about your audience. Even in informal speech, you may talk differently depending on whom you're talking to. You wouldn't use the same language with your mother-in-law as you would with your six-year-old daughter. You wouldn't speak to your grandmother the same way you would to your best friend.

In the same vein, it's important to be genuine. If you have a teenage audience, don't try to use trendy new phrases if you don't use them in real life. People can see right through that, and you may lose their trust if you seem hokey.

Another way to be casual is to tell stories and analogies. Good marketing is really just a fancy word for storytelling. And stories will always beef up your personality.

The human brain has a strong tendency to lose focus. It's estimated that we engage in up to 2,000 daydreams a day and spend up to half our waking time wandering. Telling your audience stories can help you overcome a bored brain. When the brain sees or hears a story, its neurons fire in the same patterns as the speaker's brain. It's easier to remember facts when they're told in story form.

Storytelling is one of the most powerful ways to breathe life into your products and services. By giving your products and services an identity, you'll take your target audience on a journey they yearn to experience. In order for your reader to form a personal connection with you, your stories **must** be real – authentic, creative, and inspirational.

Have some fun. Talk to your reader in a way that comes across as being natural even in your storytelling. People want to read copy that makes them feel comfortable. As if they know you.

Talk to your reader as if you were sitting across their dining room table from them or enjoying a beer with a couple of buddies.

If you really want to attract, convert, and keep more clients, be genuine. Be yourself. Be real.

7 Tips To Writing With More Personality

The problem for most people is that being "real" in print is hard for them to pull off. If you want your personality to come out in your copy, you have to write like you talk. Here are a few tips to writing with more personality.

Tip #1: Record your thoughts.

Use your smartphone or tablet. They all have recording features these days. Instead of sitting down in front of your computer, push the 'record' button on your phone, and say what you'd say if your prospect were standing in front of you. Close your eyes. Picture yourself actually talking to one person… the person you would like to be reading your letter. Take a few deep breaths. Get in a relaxed, comfortable state, and start talking. Don't edit your words. Let your thoughts come out naturally. You can edit your copy later.

It may be awkward at first, but you'll quickly get the hang of it. It won't be long and your words will begin to flow naturally. For most people, it's much easier to talk with personality than to write a letter with personality. So start with talking.

When appropriate, use analogies and metaphors that fit your audience.

After you record, transcribe your recording. Remove all the "ums", "ahs", and "errs". You'll now have a letter that's an extension of your personality. Be sure to follow the formula for a great sales letter in Chapter 4 using your transcribed draft.

When you finish your conversation, rewind and review what you said and how you said it. Was there compassion, enthusiasm, and flexibility in your voice?

This will determine exactly what type of personality you have. That's the personality you need to put into your writing and communication. That's a big part of "writing with personality".

Tip #2: Don't be boring.

Bore your reader, even for a few seconds, and they'll be gone.

A good way to avoid boring your reader is to get to the point. Don't be too long-winded. Say what you've got to say, but don't ramble. It's no different than when you're talking to someone at a social event. Their stories never seem to have an end. They're like the Energizer Bunny, they keep going... and going... and going.

Don't be too predictable. Surprise your reader now and again. Keep them on their toes.

Use short words and short sentences.

Never ramble on about your products or services. We're all proud of our businesses, but our prospects and clients only want to know one thing… "What's in it for them." ALWAYS LIVE IN YOUR PROSPECT'S WORLD.

When in doubt, tell a quick story. People love to hear a good, compelling story. That's what good marketing is all about – your ability to tell the story of your business.

Tip #3: Use common phrases your audience will understand.

Talk to them in their voice. As I mentioned earlier, make sure you are using appropriate language for your specific audience. That doesn't mean change who you are or be fake, but if you're talking to a group of senior citizens, imagine what kind of words and phrases you would use with your own grandpa. If you're speaking to a group of colleagues, write accordingly.

Tip #4: Always read your copy out loud to see if it feels good.

If it doesn't sound good out loud, you're probably not writing in your voice. Forget about the rules of grammar at this stage (after all, those rules don't really apply to the spoken word). If something reads fake or unauthentic, reword it until it feels comfortable to you.

Tip #5: Be sure to talk to one person.

Everybody wants to feel special and singled out. This doesn't have to be awkward. You can make your prospect feel special simply by writing as if you're talking to that one person instead of a large group. As you speak and/or write, imagine one person you know who could be in the target audience. Write to that person.

Tip #6: Have an opinion.

It's okay to have an opinion. The reason people are attracted to you is because of your personality. Use it to your advantage. Without opinions, nobody will ever be able to relate to you, which is really the end goal of writing with personality. Don't be afraid to put your true feelings out to the world. That's when people will feel attracted to you.

Don't worry about whether someone will agree with what you say or like you. Just be honest about how you really feel about things, but at the same time stay positive.

Tip #7: Practice by reading books by authors you enjoy.

Make note of writers who hold your attention… the ones you can't get enough of. Think about why they appeal to you. Perhaps you can infuse some of their spirit into your own writing.

You'll Soon Be Talking To Your Audience In A Warm, Friendly, Casual Way

Once in a while we all come across an article or someone's website, and the copy almost reads itself. Sentences are short. There are no hard-to-understand words. The copy flows like a powerful river. The copy is written from one person to another, as if the writer were talking to a friend in an informal setting. That's what you want to strive for when you write.

I cannot emphasize this enough. Your personality is what

will hold your reader. They're begging to "feel" who you really are. They don't want to hear from another phony salesperson who talks to them like everybody else.

Don't get too pitchy. The moment your reader feels like you're trying to pull the wool over their eyes, you're toast. Your reader will be gone in a flash.

Are you ready? Are your words clear and concise? Do they flow well? Once you've determined your distinct personality traits, you'll find it so much easier to get your message across.

Another great advantage to writing with personality is it's an instant rapport builder. Any businessperson knows without rapport, there's no foundation for gaining customers' trust. By showing your personality through your business, you're opening up and letting people see you, as a real person, and not just another business in the community.

Ask any consumer, whether for products or services, and they'll tell you the main thing they're looking for is trust. They want to trust the person they're doing business with. Trust goes a long way in the world of business these days. Every great salesperson will tell you nothing happens in the sales process until trust is established.

Keep in mind that your average prospect wakes up each morning next to a *boring* spouse... eats a *boring* breakfast... drives off in their *boring* car on a *boring* drive to their *boring* job... works with *boring* people in a *boring* office... eats a *boring* lunch... comes back home in their *boring* car to their *boring* house... you get my point.

Can you guess what the problem is? If you said boredom, you guessed right.

Promise yourself that you won't be a participant in that boring world. Start writing your sales letters and website copy with more "personality sizzle", and watch your business take off.

Remember, the amount of personality and emotion your copy carries will depend on what you say and *how* you say it (the words you choose in your copy). Choose the right words, and your copy will feel highly personal, your prospect will become more emotional when reading it, and they'll be far more likely to respond in this intense emotional state.

CHAPTER 6
Lead Generation

Leads are the lifeblood of your business. Your business cannot survive without a steady flow of good, strong, qualified leads.

Many small business owners still believe the best way, and often the only way, to find leads is the old-fashioned way of cold-call prospecting. Cold calling works, but who in the world enjoys it?

The sad reality is most business owners miss out on a huge opportunity to create their own leads. I'm talking about real leads. Truly qualified leads. Not like all those worthless leads sold by faceless companies on the Internet.

Whenever I think of cold-call prospecting, it reminds me of the movie *Glengarry Glen Ross*. In my opinion, it's one of the greatest sales movies of all time. If you haven't seen it, it's about a handful of top-notch salesmen. Their jobs are to sell remote properties in Florida, Arizona and other resort/retirement locations to prospective buyers. These guys are the "crème de la crème" of salesmen. The casting was perfect. Listen to this line up of superstars – Al Pacino, Jack Lemmon, Kevin Spacey, Alan Arkin, Ed Harris, and Alec Baldwin.

Their lives depend on strong, qualified leads. Without them, they're sunk. I recommend you set aside a couple of hours and prepare to have your eyes opened to the importance of having qualified leads in your business. This movie will definitely get your attention.

Working Smarter

There's a much better and smarter way to grow your business than cold calling. Let me give you an example. I live in Florida, so let's use one of the most popular and competitive industries in my state: pest control.

At any given time, I can pick up my local newspaper, search the Internet, or just about anywhere else, and find an endless supply of pest control ads. For the sake of this example, let's say today is the day I've decided to take care of my nagging pest control problem.

Let's see, where do I start my research? Eeny, meeny, miny, moe. For starters, I can Google "Pest Control" on my computer or smartphone. I can thumb through my recent stack of Valpak coupons. I can check my local newspaper. Whatever I do, I'll be sure to find plenty of ads for pest control.

If I find 100 ads, one thing is certain. Every one of the ads will pretty much look the same. They all have the standard company logo and business name. They usually include a catchy company slogan or something about how long they've been at the same location. At the bottom of the page, there's usually an offer for a free estimate, and of course, their promise to fix my bug issue.

There's just one problem – and it's a biggie. They're all cookie-cutter ads. Every single one of them looks alike.

This problem is not unique to the pest control industry. From an advertising standpoint, it's at an epidemic level. You name the industry, and 99.9% of the advertising is the same... the car industry, law offices, dentists, plumbers, veterinarians, chiropractors, insurance agencies... You name the industry. They ALL look alike.

The overwhelming majority of businesses advertise the same way. They do the same exact thing as their competitors. It's "tombstone" advertising. Their ads look just like a big business card – or a headstone.

To get your prospect's attention, your advertising MUST be different. You must stand out and show up like nobody else. You cannot simply list your services or talk about how you're a great family business. At this point in the process, nobody cares.

A more effective approach is to advertise from your prospective customer's point of view. Consumer awareness marketing is the easiest way to get noticed and build trust with your prospects. It starts by "flipping the switch" and taking the focus off of you. Instead, you offer something of value to your prospects.

Here's the psychology behind this approach. At its core, effective marketing is applied psychology. Back in the early 1950s, the great marketer and copywriter, Robert Collier, said, **"As a marketer, your goal is to enter the conversation already going on in your prospect's mind."**

Your prospects are thinking, "I don't know to choose this company. I don't know anything about this product or service." That's the point where you want to join their thoughts and answer those critical concerns. I refer to this process as "education-based" marketing.

There was a book written years ago called *The Book Of Survival*. There's a quote in the book that says, "To live through a difficult situation, you don't need the reflexes of a grand prix driver, the muscles of a Hercules, or the mind of an Einstein. You simply need to know *what* to do."

In order to generate more business, you don't need to be a genius, you just need to know *what* to do so people will pay attention to you... and buy from you.

Take the attention off of you and put it on your prospect. Instead of saying, "I'm the best widget maker in town, and I'm the guy you should be doing business with," turn all that focus 180 degrees to your prospect. They have important questions they want answered. Your prospects are not interested in your logo or your business. They want to know what you can do for them.

Why You Should Stop Cold-Call Prospecting

Can you build a profitable business making cold calls your entire career? Absolutely you can. However, you better have mighty thick skin, plenty of time, shoe leather, and the ability to handle constant rejection.

A better question to ask yourself is why you would subject yourself to a life sentence of cold-call prospecting, especially if you knew about an age-old, tested-and-proven marketing strategy that makes cold-call prospecting obsolete. That would be like a farmer insisting on breaking his back every day, plowing his 40 acres of crops with a hand spade, knowing he had a brand new tractor in the barn.

To better illustrate my point, let me ask you a question. Let's say you wanted to catch some birds. How would you do it? Would you get a net and take off into the woods? Or would you build a birdcage and try to catch one bird at a time? Those ideas might work. However, there's no guarantee they will, and even if they did, you'd likely wear yourself out.

Consider this option. Instead of trying to chase or trap a single bird, what if instead, you built a "bird-feeder" that attracted hundreds of birds? A safe-haven, stocked with plenty of food and water in an environment protected from dangerous predators. A place with the freedom to come and go as they pleased without fear of being caught or killed.

Do you think you might attract more birds that way? Of course you would. It's a no-brainer. Birds are just like people. They're intuitive. They can sense the difference between being chased and attracted. They know the difference between danger and opportunity.

Your prospects are "attracted" to you instead of being "chased", which raises you above your competition. The wolves are out there in the marketplace dressed in sheep's clothing, stalking their prey, driven by the greed of a needed commission check.

A properly designed lead generation system provides a place where your prospects can feel safe, free to come and go as they please, on their terms. A place they can gather valuable, helpful information... until they're ready to buy. It's your version of a bird feeder. Distrust is replaced by trust and respect.

In case you were wondering, there is NO industry, business, or niche where a properly constructed lead generation system will not work. Let me say that again. There is <u>NO</u> industry a properly designed lead-generation system will NOT work. You just have to match the **right** bait to the **right** audience and deliver it the **right** way.

From now on, your focus should be on creating lead-generating ads, which include attention-getting headlines. Make your ads stand out by *not* focusing on you or your business. Instead, focus on educating your prospect. Start thinking like them. Ask yourself:

- What are your prospects thinking about as they prepare to buy what you sell?
- What questions are your prospects constantly asking themselves?

When you're able to answer those questions, your prospect will begin to hold you in high esteem. With that information, put some material together and give it away for free.

Before most consumers make a purchase, especially a big one, they're likely to do research. If you're the one who provides those answers, you're going to have an advantage over your competitors. People will be more likely to request a free report with that kind of information before they'll respond to a typical ad.

This strategy will work for any type of business, industry, or niche. Come up with a report or **Consumer Awareness Guide. Give it a compelling title. For example:**

- **How To Avoid The 4 Major Rip-Offs Of** _____

- **7 Costly Misconceptions About** _____

- **9 Mistakes To Avoid When Hiring A** _____

- **3 Steps To** _____

Most people want to avoid pitfalls, mistakes, and rip-offs. Rather than promoting your business, instead offer a FREE eBook, a FREE Consumer Awareness Guide, or a FREE audio, or DVD… or any combination of these things.

Using the pest control industry from my earlier example, what if you ran a lead-generation ad with a big headline that said something like, *"Don't Call A Pest Control Company Until You Read Our Free Consumer Awareness Guide – The 7 Biggest Insider Secrets The Pest Control Industry Hopes You Never Discover"*?

Or, a financial planner could offer a free report titled *"5*

Secrets The IRS Hopes You NEVER Discover That Can Save The Typical Family At Least $2,000 A Year In Taxes."

Or, a widget-maker could advertise *"Free Report And Audio CD Reveals: How To _____ So That _____ Goes Away."* Simply fill in the blanks appropriate for your niche or industry.

Do you see how a free report like this can help attract the people you want to do business with, and, at the same time, eliminate those you *don't* want as clients? By solving a perplexing problem, you'll attract interest.

Consumers want answers to their problems. They want to know "secrets". They want to "discover" something. Help them do that. Give them what they want, and you'll be seen completely differently than your competitors.

An ad like those in the above examples will set you apart from your competitors. Instead of making your ad about your *business*, make it about your *prospect*.

Do you see what just happened here? You've completely eliminated selling from the sales process. Instead, you've become a "problem solver"… a "trusted advisor". You've gone from being a pest to a welcomed guest.

The Science Of Lead Generation

Most small business owners spend their entire careers doing what their competitors do. We really can't take all the blame. We grew up with that mindset. It's been hammered into our brains for years. After all, the big boys like Coke, Nike, and Toyota have always advertised that way. Big banks, insurance companies, and technical and industrial corporations do the same. They have huge budgets, millions of advertising dollars to promote their brand. They're telling their audience, "We've been here a 100 years, and we'll be here another 100 years.

Come buy from us when you're ready."

You and I can't do that. It would be a certain death sentence to advertise like big companies. You'd be eaten alive by your competition.

I learned this lesson the hard way. When I started my business, I tried to use the same "brand" marketing strategies I learned when I was in the marketing division for Delta Air Lines. Trying to market my company like one of the big boys almost cost me my business.

As small business owners, our marketing objectives are much simpler. Our goal is to spend $1.00 today and get $2.00, or $20.00, back tomorrow. We can't afford to spend years building "good will" with brand identity. That's not to say "good will" wouldn't be a nice by-product. But, we both know we don't have the time to wait for good will to kick in; we can't buy groceries with good will.

Lead generation marketing not only changes the way you market your business, it allows you to accurately track and measure everything you do. You'll know instantly what's working, and what isn't.

Lead Generation Has 6 Simple, Tested & Proven Rules

From now on, every ad you run, every letter or postcard you mail, every website you put up, every email you write <u>MUST</u> adhere to the following "hard and fast" direct marketing rules. <u>Stick to these rules – no matter what</u>. Keep your business on this strict, direct-marketing diet for at least six months. Then get ready because your business is going to take off!

1. Always Have An Offer

Everything you do must have a "Call to Action". Ask

your prospect to do something to take action. Never just advertise and say, "Hi, here I am. If you ever decide to buy a widget, I'm a great widget-maker. Why not do business with me?"

Ask yourself, "What is it my prospect wants to know? What's on their mind? What do they want to hear?"

Keep in mind that your prospects don't care as much about your business as you do. At this point in the sales process, they could care less about how long you've been in business or how long you've been at the same location, or how many alphabet letters you have after your name. None of that means a hill of beans to them. All they want to know is *"What's In It For Me?* (WIIFM) They want to know how you're going to solve THEIR problem. And they want to know how you're going to do it better, and differently, than your competitors.

Nothing else matters to them at this point.

2. Always Have A Reason For Your Prospect To Respond Right Now

Your offer must compel your potential clients or referral sources to contact you. Your goal is immediate response. A plain-vanilla offer won't do it. For example, if you legally can do so in your state, offer a certain dollar amount off closing costs with an expiring deadline, or offer loans with attractive rates and terms for a certain time period.

Your goal is to get consumers to respond when they see your ad, not to merely "think about it" indefinitely.

3. Always Provide Clear Instructions On How To Respond

Any marketing piece – whether it's an ad, flier, sales

letter, website or phone script – should lead prospective clients or referral sources to take action. That is, you must tell them exactly what you want them to do, how and when you want them to do it, and what will happen when they do.

Don't send anything that doesn't have clear instructions.

4. Always Have Accurate Tracking And Measurement

Once you begin measuring and tracking your campaigns, you'll know precisely what's working and what isn't. You'll be able to quickly drop campaigns that fizzle. You'll be able to double-down on campaigns that make your phone ring or create a surge of "opt-ins" on your website. Your marketing will become scientific because you'll eliminate waste and guesswork. If something you do lays an egg, drop it like a hot potato and say, "Next".

The buying process has changed, and marketers need to find new ways to be heard among the increasing noise. Instead of locating customers with mass marketing and email blasts, focus on being found using lead-generation marketing. This will help you build continuous relationships with buyers.

In the next section, we'll discuss some ways to track and measure your success.

5. Always Have Accurate Follow-up

If someone reads your ad and calls your office to ask a question, make sure the person receiving the call does something with that opportunity. That staff person should capture the caller's name, address, and e-mail address and offer to schedule an appointment or provide more information.

Next, put those names on your monthly newsletter mailing list. If you don't publish a monthly newsletter, it's time to start. It likely will be one of the most read pieces of direct mail you send. We'll cover newsletters in greater detail in Chapter 7. Follow up regularly. The money is in your follow-up. Sadly most people give up too easily at this point.

6. Always Have Strong Sales Copy With Plenty Of Personality

There is enormous, overwhelming competition for your customer's attention. <u>Always use compelling copy in your marketing materials</u>.

For instance, sell yourself as a "wizard" who possesses the "magical solutions" to consumers' challenges. Use personality in your copy; don't focus solely on your products and services like everyone else does.

Draw attention to yourself and to your positioning as the expert in a particular niche. You can't be all things to all people, so don't try. **Be a specialist,** not a generalist.

It is essential you devise a marketing system that attracts good leads, repels bad leads, screens leads, pre-sells leads and has people wanting to meet or talk with you about your offer. And always remember: Features rarely sell. <u>Only benefits applied directly to consumers actually matter to them</u>.

Tracking And Measurement

Before you launch any direct marketing campaign, set a system in place that will allow you to track the results. Tracking and measuring your results means you can see what gets a response from your prospects and clients, what gets the most interaction, and what leads to the most sales, sign-ups, or other action.

You then have the critical data you need to focus on what

works and to save money by eliminating marketing that doesn't work. Ask any successful direct-marketer, and they'll all tell you. Test, test, test. With today's technology, you can test different headlines and messages at the same time. You'll also get feedback quickly so you'll know what's working and what isn't.

Marketing metrics play an important role in understanding how effective your campaigns are. The metric that top marketers live and die by is response rate – the percentage of potential customers who take the next step in the purchasing process. Typical response rates run between one and two percent, though it can be higher depending on your offer and target market. When you know your response rate, you can test and tweak different marketing materials to achieve greater success; the following lists 10 easy ways to track marketing response rate:

1. Physical Coupons: Coupons are among the longest-standing and most effective ways to track response rates. You can print direct-mail postcards, brochures, flyers, and other marketing materials with perforated tear-away coupons; or, print business cards and rack cards as coupons. Then count how many coupons are redeemed to determine your response rate.

2. Coupon Codes: Coupon codes are excellent ways to track response rate, particularly for direct mail and online marketing campaigns. Coupon codes can be automatically counted so you can measure response at a glance.

3. Variable URLs: Variable URLs are web addresses created for specific customers. For example, let's say you launch a direct mail postcard marketing campaign that directs customers to your website to make a purchase or complete some other action. Your customer will be given a personalized URL, such as www.YOURSITE.COM/FIRSTNAME-LASTNAME. This type of personalization can help motivate customers to respond and also makes it very easy to track response rate.

4. QR Codes: QR codes remain popular ways to drive traffic to your website, mobile apps, and social media pages. Many services offer dynamic QR codes, which allow you to change the page redirects for a single QR code and provide valuable analytics.

5. Landing Page Analytics: Every website should have analytics installed so you know how customers are interacting with your content. The best marketing campaigns send customers to dedicated campaign-specific landing pages that aren't promoted elsewhere. By combining the power of custom landing pages with analytics, you can quickly see how many customers are responding to your postcards, posters, flyers, and other marketing materials. Google Analytics is one of the most popular free apps for tracking website visitors. It offers a comprehensive overview of visitor demographics, page visits, and more.

6. Email Analytics: Similarly, email marketing campaigns should include measurable analytical data so you can see how many email recipients open your emails, how many click, and what they do once they arrive on your landing page. Most major email services offer built-in analytics. I use AWeber (www.aweber.com), but there are many companies that offer email services to help you attract and improve response rates.

7. Phone Calls: It might seem old school, but this is one of the best ways to measure response – especially if your marketing materials specifically request customers to call a number.

8. Foot Traffic: Similarly, monitoring foot traffic at your brick-and-mortar location can be effective. If you compare the number of people who visit your storefront during a particular campaign to the number of people who typically visit your storefront, you can easily measure your response rate to that campaign.

9. Emails/Contact Form Submissions: Another easy way to measure response rate is to count the number of emails or contact form submissions you receive during a campaign versus your averages. This is especially effective if you've asked customers to fill out a contact form or newsletter subscription form, or to email you directly to receive more information.

10. Purchases: Finally, you can track response by counting the number of purchases made during your campaign.

All of these methods can be used to determine your response rates, but those that measure real campaign-specific numbers are the most accurate: coupons and coupon codes. For example, <u>it's important to remove assumptions from the equation so you can make educated decisions based on real data</u>.

How Lead Generation Works

In Chapter 4, we talked about the fisherman, who instead of thinking like the other fishermen, thought like the fish. When you "think" like your prospect and match the right bait to the right audience, you *will* attract leads. That's because we all make buying decisions the same way. We're hardwired that way. It's part of our DNA. You put the right bait in front of the right prospects, and they'll take it. **Even better, your competitors won't have a clue how to compete with you.**

You'll turn invisible prospects into visible, warm leads by getting people to raise their hands and identify themselves. They'll tell you they're interested, at least at some level, in what you're trying to sell them. That's gold to any business owner.

At this critical point, you make an exchange with your prospect.

Your prospect gets what they want, and you get what *you* want, which in this case, is their email address. At this point, their name gets added to an automated email system called an "auto-responder". We'll talk more about the incredible power of auto-responders in Chapter 12.

In the meantime, your prospect will read, listen, or watch what you gave them. The information is your golden opportunity to showcase your knowledge and expertise. Your prospects think you've given them a report or information. In reality, it's much more than that. <u>You've put in their hands a very powerful sales letter, in disguise</u>.

Think about that for a minute. You've given your prospect valuable help and information, without having to sell or pitch anything. You haven't pressured them or asked them to make a quick purchase decision. You've done the opposite.

Instead of being like a traditional salesperson, you're seen as someone who has taken the time to educate, inform, and provide help. <u>The more information you share, the more your prospects begin to trust you</u>.

Best of all, your lead-generation system is completely automated. You can be anywhere... in your office working, at home, asleep in bed, or sitting on the beach in Tahiti sipping a

Piña Colada. Your system doesn't care where you are. That's because it's on autopilot, sifting and sorting, attracting and qualifying all of your prospects, 24/7. Your prospects could *care* less where you are. They're happy. They received the information they wanted, delivered to them on "their terms", in helpful, bite-sized pieces. And, most importantly, they got the information they wanted *without* having to talk to a live salesperson.

In essence, you've turned the world of traditional sales on its ears.

Good work. Take a bow.

Here's another thing that makes lead generation appealing to your target audience. Consumers LOVE to buy stuff. What they don't like is being pressured to buy things by pushy salespeople. **A lead-generation system solves that problem because it eliminates high-pressure sales**. It puts your prospect in the driver's seat because it gives them full control to move through the sales process at *their* pace, on *their* terms.

During this process, resistance begins to slowly melt away. Trust grows, and you go from the individual they don't want to hear from, to the expert they now have great respect for. In time, a high percentage of your leads will be predisposed, predetermined, and prequalified to do business with you, and in most cases, with price resistance off the table.

CHAPTER 7
Newsletter Magic

I'm pretty sure it's a safe bet you know who Superman is. Superman disguised himself as Clark Kent, the mild-mannered reporter for a great metropolitan newspaper. That's right. He worked at the *Daily Planet*, the largest newspaper in Metropolis. Why do you think he chose a newspaper? Because that's the place everyone goes to find out what's happening. What better way to keep your finger on the pulse of what's happening?

Imagine if your business had its own "Daily Planet". Many of my clients do. It's called "The Newsletter". It's your own publication that goes out each and every month to your clients and prospects, without fail.

Newsletters are not perceived in the same manner as are postcards, fliers, or other forms of direct mail marketing. When people receive these or anything else that has a sales and marketing feel to it, their guard goes up and they think, "Uh-oh. What are they trying to sell me?"

Newsletters work well because they're read as informational pieces, making them more welcome when they are received. As such, they have higher readership than other forms of advertising. People also tend to be more receptive to what you have to say in your newsletter because newsletters aren't meant to be sales tools. Rather, they are designed to be a resource.

At the beginning of this book, I mentioned three

marketing pillars that highly successful businesses constantly strive to master. I refer to these pillars as **"Attract 'em"**, **"Convert 'em"**, and **"Keep 'em"**.

In order to effectively market your business, you must **attract** prospects with something that compels them to take some kind of action. Usually that **attraction** comes by giving something away, for free – valuable, helpful information like a free report, eBook, audio, or DVD. Education-based information compels your prospects to respond and take action. It will also separate you from your competitors. To advertise otherwise is a huge waste of your marketing dollars.

Effective marketing is about being consistent and showing up like nobody else. To do anything less will cause your prospects and clients to view you as a "commodity."

Producing a monthly newsletter is a perfect example of this form of marketing. You'll **"attract"** prospects by being friendly, helpful, and trustworthy. Your consistency will help build trust in an untrusting world, which will ultimately lead to **"converting"** them into loyal customers.

Once you've **attracted** prospects, and eventually **converted** them into customers and clients, you're poised to **keep** them over the long haul.

Many businesses do the first two parts okay but fail miserably to do the little things to build long-term loyalty. Once they "sell" something to a customer, they think their job is over. Not so. That's just the beginning. Effective marketing doesn't stop there. The lifetime value to a client over the long haul can be substantial.

Top marketers know that it costs 6-7 times more money to get a new client than it does to keep one. When you think long term, you increase the odds of **keeping** customers and clients for years to come. The accumulative effect can be staggering.

There's no better way to put the **"attract 'em"**, **"convert 'em", **"keep 'em"** marketing system in full swing, than producing your own printed monthly newsletter.

Maximizing The "Attract 'em," "Covert 'em," "Keep 'em" Formula

Now I want to ask you one of those hard, thought-provoking questions. Why wouldn't you want to keep in touch with your clients and nurture your relationships with them every month? If you don't have a good answer, pay close attention to what I'm about to share with you, as it will likely be the single best thing you do for your business.

I don't care if you're a business owner, a solopreneur, or run a business with hundreds of employees. You can be a realtor, a painter, a plumber, a dentist, or a clock maker. It doesn't matter. The same principles apply.

Allow me to set the record straight about something I've personally experienced over the last 17 years. As a freelance copywriter and marketing consultant, I've had the privilege of writing marketing campaigns for hundreds of highly successful business owners in many niches and industries. And, in every case, the businesses are at the top in their respective fields. Their businesses run like machines. Their marketing is strong and consistent. <u>Almost to a person, they all produce a monthly newsletter</u>. Many have their own books, and in some cases, have authored several. **In almost every case, their monthly printed newsletter is the anchor to their marketing.**

My friend and long-time client, Brian Fricke, says, "If you took away everything I do from a marketing perspective except one thing, I would want to keep my monthly client newsletter."

Success leaves clues. These folks aren't spending a lot of time and money every month on something that doesn't work –

and work well. As you read the rest of this chapter, if you're not sure a monthly newsletter would be a good move for you, dump that thought. You can do it yourself or get someone else to handle it for you – but make sure you get a newsletter on your "to do" list immediately. It's that important.

So, if a printed monthly newsletter is powerful, why don't more business owners have one? Good question. I have my reasons:

People are lazy. Putting together a monthly newsletter is no easy task. It takes a lot of time, work, and elbow grease.

Lack of discipline. Plenty of business owners have given newsletters a shot. They put one or two editions together, and when they don't get immediate results, they throw in the towel. If you're going to think like that, don't start a newsletter.

Difficulty meeting deadlines. You can't let your deadline pass on a newsletter. It's like your mini version of the *Daily Planet*. Things have to get done, edited, and out the door on time, EVERY MONTH.

Inability to write good copy. Newsletter writing is personal and conversational. There's definitely a formula to writing newsletter articles. Writing with clarity is not the easiest thing to do. But like anything else this important, it's worth learning, or outsourcing to someone who knows how to do it.

Why You Should Produce A Monthly Newsletter

Your newsletter is a great reminder. Yes, that's right. It reminds your clients and prospects *who* you are and *what* you do. In fact, not everybody will read your newsletter every month. That's okay. They'll still be reminded about you every time they open their mailbox.

Your newsletter will position you as an expert. People

would much prefer to work with an expert. For example, if you needed surgery, who would you rather put your trust in… a surgeon who was a specialist or a general practitioner? I think the answer is obvious. You'd want the best. You'd want a specialist.

An expert.

Your newsletter makes you "the expert". It will help you establish stronger positioning in your marketplace. It's no secret that people like to buy from those they know, like, and trust. Every time a prospect or client reads your newsletter, your credibility goes up a notch, and you never want to miss out on a potential sale.

Quick story. About five years ago, I had my kitchen remodeled. The guy did an outstanding job. Several friends complemented me on the quality of his work. A few even asked for his phone number. I couldn't help them because I'd lost contact with the guy. Too bad, because I could' have sent him a ton of business. A simple, monthly newsletter would have solved that problem. Unfortunately millions of small businesses do the same thing. They work like dogs to earn someone's trust. But then, when the sale is done, they do absolutely nothing to maintain that relationship. What a waste.

Newsletters are also a great way to announce new services and create up-sells, referrals, and lead generation opportunities. The more your prospects and clients hear from you, the more they'll trust you and see you as the expert in your market. You'll begin to connect with your clients and prospects on a much deeper level. The people who get your newsletter every month will get used to hearing from you. And the more you put your personal stamp on it, the more they'll feel a connection with you. And, since you're the editor, you'll have full control to make that happen. Think about it. Who else in your niche or industry gets to arrive in your clients' and prospects' mailboxes every month and spend one-on-one time with them? It's a huge advantage – the ultimate soft sell. Besides, people love reading interesting things and getting something of value for free. Not only will they remember the articles, they'll remember *where* they read them and look forward to more interesting information in the coming months.

We have one client who started with a simple, fold-over, two-page newsletter. He now produces a 16-page, multi-color newsletter with inserts. He's become a regular Perry White. He credits part of his business's success to his newsletter.

Much research has been done about its many benefits. Here are just a few of the benefits:

- A newsletter is a powerful way to showcase your company's reputation. It's one of the most effective ways to increase lead generation.
- A newsletter will increase the lifetime value of your clients.
- Newsletters are cost efficient. They're also a cost-effective way to "touch" your clients every month and have a personal conversation with them. And the best part, your reader will decide when it's best for them to read it, unlike an email newsletter likely to arrive in their email inbox in the middle of a busy day.
- Your newsletter leverages your marketing efforts.
- Your newsletter provides instantaneous trackable results.
- Your newsletter will open opportunities for your clients to easily and immediately interact with you.
- Your newsletter will create a higher response rate because it is being sent to a more receptive audience.
- Your newsletter is for your client's "eyes only". Unlike social media and other types of advertising, your competitors will have NO idea what you're sharing with

your other customers, clients, or patients.

- Your newsletter will be perceived as a publication, not as advertising. It's a friendly, non-evasive way to connect and build rapport.
- Your monthly printed newsletter has tremendous "pass-along" value. Since it's printed, people can share it with friends, family, neighbors, and colleagues. It's one of the best ways to build a powerful referral culture for your business.
- Your newsletter is a great way to make someone smile by sharing uplifting stories and short articles that help build rapport with your readers. Think of it as your version of a *Readers Digest*.

Tips To Help You Produce A Successful Newsletter

There's a loose formula to creating your own newsletter. (See two examples on pages 131-132.) Here are some tips:

- Make it about your customers, clients, patients and prospects, not you. Live in *their* world.
- The title of your newsletter should be "industry related". For example: One of our clients is a rising star in the real estate market in her area. She named her newsletter "Front Porch News". Her articles are mostly based around the real estate field. Much of her content covers gardening, baking, lawn care, decorating, etc. She mails her newsletter every month to her constantly growing database of new and existing clients.
- Newsletters are about content. Your articles should be inviting, interesting, and informative. People miss the human touch. The right article can move anyone. They also must be content rich. People love something of value

for free.

Once you start sending a monthly newsletter, you cannot stop. Your marketing and advertising budget is an item that must be on your list of monthly costs. The newsletter is exactly the same. You can't decide to do a newsletter part time or when you feel like it. Once you start publishing, it's full speed ahead. No sidetracks, no gaps. It's definitely one of your "long haul" marketing commitments, but it will be more than worth it.

Newsletters can be self-promoting too. If three people are standing around the coffee pot in the break room at work, often a conversation starts about current events and the latest news. Usually, the first thing you hear someone say is, "I read in the *Times* today," or, "I saw an article in the *Post*." People like to use the source of information before they deliver the information. It gives credence and meaning to the information they're about to give. Don't be surprised if one day people at one of your accounts is saying, "I read in Acme's newsletter today..." It happens to others. It can happen for you.

There's another advantage to publishing a newsletter. Imagine a salesperson making cold calls once a month to your prospective clients or customers. Rain or shine, they're going in on that cold call, once a month, without fail. Something like that would have to be beneficial. However, what would it cost you?

The answer is... plenty.

Your newsletter is like that "cold-call salesperson". It can be sitting on the corner of a decision maker's desk, waiting to be read. Every month it shows up. It doesn't call in sick. It doesn't complain or take vacations. More importantly, it costs a mere fraction of what you'd have to pay a sales rep.

Your newsletter format is up to you. However, most folks like to use a "column" format. That's about the closest look you'll get to give your newsletter that newspaper or magazine feel. It seems to be easiest on the eyes. That's why newspapers use it. However, it's your periodical. Do what you feel works best for you. Just make sure your newsletter has your "look and feel" stamped on it. Articles, design, layout, and branding should have your unique fingerprint.

We have countless stories and case studies of business owners who've enjoyed the surge of new referrals and revenues from their newsletters.

Your newsletter will be successful if you remember the basics. Use articles that "attract" and don't "repel" your readers. For example, if it's allergy season, make sure there's an article about how to avoid pollen and stay in air conditioning.

Almost every month has a holiday in it. Be sure there's an article about that holiday. Recipes are usually a big hit. Remember, this is all about your prospects and clients, not you and your business.

Avoid that urge to advertise your business too much. It's okay to have an insert, or to subtly plug a new product or service from time to time. But for the most part, make it about your reader. Make it neighborly and friendly. That's where you'll see your biggest results. Keep it informative. As long as your newsletter follows this philosophy, your readers will see it as something *for them*, and they'll be sure to remember it came *from you*.

As your newsletter grows, you might be able to add sponsors to offset your investment. This is a great place to sell advertising. If you provide enough value to your industry, you'll be able to charge a small monthly subscription. It would be a nice feeling to wake up the first of every month knowing within reason you can count on a certain number of subscribers to automatically buy your newsletter.

Your newsletter is an excellent place to throw in an occasional "perk" or surprise. For example, you can provide a CD with information that might be deemed helpful to your audience. You can come up with all kinds of additional bonuses that take people to your website to track and measure response.

There's probably a good group of customers out there who want to know when your new product line launches, or they want to know which conference you'll be speaking at next… all items that continue to build a relationship with your audience.

A monthly newsletter is a key component to staying in touch with the people who want to stay in touch with you. Keeping yourself and your business, in front of your clients and prospects, every single month!

CHAPTER 8
Turn Features Into Benefits

To most people, the word "incest" conjures up awful thoughts. As a small business owner, you may be guilty of 'marketing incest'. That's when you advertise and market your business like every other business you compete with. In human culture, inbreeding dumbs people down. Most small businesses are incestuous in that they're resistant to outside influence or change. Instead, they look around, see what their competitors are doing, and simply copy them. It's a process of the blind leading the blind. To be blunt, everybody gets stupider and stupider.

There's absolutely no innovation.

This is extremely important because effective marketing requires you to separate yourself from everybody else. To avoid being a victim of 'marketing incest', you must differentiate yourself.

Features Tell, Benefits Sell. It was Charles Revson (the pioneering cosmetics industry executive who created and managed Revlon Cosmetics through five decades) who clearly understood and practiced this marketing principle when he said, "In the factory we make cosmetics; in the drugstore we sell hope."

Another oft-quoted marketing lesson is from Theodore Levitt who once told his M.B.A. students at Harvard, "People don't want to buy a quarter-inch drill. They want a quarter-inch hole."

Always ask yourself: What makes your company and services different from your competitors? What makes you stand out? What are you doing to differentiate yourself from your competitors? The answers are vital to your long-term success. If you don't have answers to these questions, now may be a good time to stop and think about this.

One of the biggest things you can do is start thinking like your prospect.

Take a minute to do it now. Make a list of your 5 strongest business features. Now, turn them around into benefits your customer will find valuable.

The Difference Between "Benefits" And "Features"

The *feature* of a fast Internet connection provides the benefit of being able to find your way when you're lost. A fast Internet connection is a 'feature', but the ability to "quickly find your way when you're lost," is a 'benefit'.

Features are defined as surface statements about your product, such as what it can do, its dimensions and specs, and so on. Benefits, by definition, show the end result of what a product can actually accomplish for the reader.

It's easy to determine what your top 5 business features are. You created it. It should be secondhand knowledge to you. Take a few minutes to make your list if you didn't in the previous section. Determining your features is the starting point.

Turning your business's features into your customer or client's benefits gives you a giant step forward in building rapport. You heard me say it earlier in this book. Rapport builds trust. And as you know, nothing happens in the sales process until trust is established.

You can turn your marketing and advertising around to

reflect the wants and needs of your customer. You're opening up the avenue to bring back that "human touch" to marketing and advertising. It all ties together. It's one person talking to another, putting *their* needs before *yours*.

Whether you're the plumber, the dentist, or the new real estate broker on the block, today may be the day someone needs your product or service. Who are they going to likely remember when they need that plumber? The one who advertised with the customer in mind. The plumber who decided to change some of his ad copy to reflect the concerns of his customers. All things being equal, consumers are going to reach out for the person they already have rapport with – the business owner who thinks like their customers.

That's going to be you.

Turning features into benefits is a huge part of any marketing and advertising campaign, not just in the world of direct response marketing. There are books galore on the subject.

If the majority of experts who write copy for a living place that kind of importance on turning features into benefits, shouldn't you?

Here's what I mean.

Let's say you've recently decided to get in shape. You want to start hiking. You know you'll need some high-quality hiking boots that will stand up to the riggers of the backcountry. So, you head down to the local hiking and outdoor store and tell the super sporty-looking salesperson what you're looking for. He lights up because he's a big hiker and knows firsthand what you need.

Full of enthusiasm, the kid tells you your best option would be the new Norwegian welt construction boots because they have a wide platform underfoot for warmth and stability. He goes on to tell you the boot insole is one piece with high-quality Tesive, 3-bar knit lining, complete with bellows tongue, and Italian craftsmanship.

Huh?

The guy lost you at Norwegian welt construction. Everything he said after that went right over your head. The kid salesman made you feel dumb to the point where you felt like reconsidering your plans to get fit again.

Sound familiar?

Of course it does. You've had it happen to you plenty of times. You may have even done it yourself. You're so proud of your products and services that you forget to think about your customers. You're so focused on the features of what you're selling, you forget to think about it from your buyer's perspective.

This example isn't limited to face-to-face sales. Not by a long shot. The Internet has allowed marketers to take their advertising mistakes online. Websites and sales letters are written the same way. The copy is full of features, specifications, and technical mumbo-jumbo. But it's mostly stuff the average buyer doesn't understand. Online and offline businesses are so focused on themselves, they forget to talk about the most important thing… what's in it for their buyer.

There's a much better, more effective way to sell and build rapport. When you turn the features of your product into benefits to a consumer, it changes everything.

For example, let's say you sell TVs. A typical ad will boast about one feature after the other, all the creature features your TV has.

Now, let's word it in a way that focuses on the customer… something like this, "Your life will be less stressful and far more relaxing. That's because you'll enjoy high definition television without having to spend more money. You won't have to worry about leaving the power on, burning energy when you're busy."

Another example. Let's say you sell high-quality windows. A typical salesperson might say, "Our windows are double paned." Again, that's a feature.

Let's turn that feature of the product into a benefit to the buyer by saying, "Since these windows are double paned, you won't *ever* be bothered by outside noises. Instead, you'll be inside your home relaxing and enjoying TV with your family."

Do you see the difference?

Here's an example for security systems. "We'll monitor your house 24/7."

A better statement: "Your alarm system won't go down. As a result, you and your loved-ones will be able to enjoy uninterrupted safety and comfort around the clock. You and everyone will sleep better with true peace of mind."

Instead of selling a car by featuring "more miles per gallon," you could say, "Your new car will generate income for you with real savings in reduced fuel consumption."

Trying to sell swimming pools? "Think of the fun memories you'll build with your family enjoying the cool, comfortable waters together."

Simply transfer the features of your product or service into benefits for your buyer. ALWAYS live in your prospect's world. When in doubt, think of the benefits to your prospect – not the features of it.

One more quick example… Instead of me saying to my clients, "I write high-converting, direct-response copy." I would say something like, "You'll benefit from more prospects attracted to your business, which will convert to new business for you."

A simple rule of thumb is – instead of focusing on your business, focus on your prospect.

Look at your current advertising both online and offline.

Go through your website and brochures. Give your business a 'writing audit' to see if you're focusing too much on the features of your products and services instead of the benefits to your clients. If it's all about you, you're leaking oil and leaving money on the table.

Real benefits connect to your customer's desires, such as saving time; reducing costs; making more money; and becoming happier, healthier, more relaxed, or more productive.

If you'd like to know more about this subject, you can download our free guide, "How to turn features into benefits and seduce your prospects into buyers." You can access it here at www.specialtymarketingconsultants.com/benefits

Now, let's go back to the hiking store example we talked about a moment ago. The super sporty sales guy is now explaining both the features of his hiking boots *and* the benefits. In his presentation, he's making sure he says things like, "These boots are so well made, even in the cold rain, your toes will feel warm and cozy. The boots have three layers of foam, so whether you're walking uphill, downhill, or on a flat surface, the results will be the same – maximum comfort to your feet. And, because of the ergonomic design, your support will remain comfortable, even after many hours of intense hiking on uneven surfaces."

Sounds better, doesn't it?

You now have a good understanding of what each feature means and what it does. The young salesman's pitch was more persuasive than when he was so focused on his product, rattling off all the technical stuff.

Practice doing this in your writing. Join the conversation going on in your prospect's mind. Find out what they secretly dream about, and then figure out how you can fulfill their wishes and desires with your product or service.

When you connect your knowhow and enthusiasm along

with your client's desires, magic things happen. Your business will grow, you'll be able to increase your fees and drop difficult clients, and have a lot more fun in the process.

CHAPTER 9
Raising The Bar

You know you've done a fairly gutsy thing. You decided that you'd go into business for yourself. If you took a close look at the mountain of statistics that show the failure rate of businesses today, you'd go back to sleep and wake up with another idea. My hat is off to you. You decided to take on the challenge.

There are quite a few successful business owners out there today, and we know how they got there – through hard work, dedication, and the will to get it done. However, there's another factor that usually gets overlooked. It's the ability not to settle. I don't mean settle as in, "We finally settled that deal." I mean, they don't settle into the status quo. Doing a good job is only one of the ingredients.

My company, Specialty Marketing Consultants, runs a 2-hour marketing and sales seminar every other Tuesday at the University of Central Florida's Business Incubator. At a recent meeting, one of the attendees asked, "Is there a difference between a business owner and an entrepreneur?" My immediate answer was, "Yes."

A business owner becomes focused on his or her business. Can I make it run more efficiently? Can I increase growth 10% this year? How can I be more profitable? All great things that must be accomplished in order to have a more successful business. But, a bigger question is…

Getting Your Business Where You Want It To Be

Are You A Business Owner Or An Entrepreneur?

Most people think these two words are interchangeable. "Business owner" and "entrepreneur".

There's a profound difference between the two though. Most of our clients come to us as business owners, and in the process, develop into entrepreneurs.

The faster you make the transition, the better off you'll be, the more money you'll make, the faster you'll make it, and the more fun you'll have in the process.

This is one of the most overlooked differences in the two terms.

Let's take a closer look at the difference. To illustrate my example, let's say our subject business owner owns a computer store. We'll say he has a store on Main Street in an average-sized town. If you were to visit with him, look around, and then come back in 3-4 years, you'd find pretty much the same business. He may have taken over the small, vacated bookstore next to him... maybe even added a specialty area or two. He may even make house calls or have another store on the other side of town.

Overall, it may be a bigger computer store. His product lines may have changed a bit. Technology will dictate that. But, for the most part, the guy is still running a computer store. And in social circles, if you were to ask him what he does, his answer will always be the same. He'll tell you he's an IT guy, or more likely, he'll tell you he owns a computer store.

Now, if he is a client of mine and works with my company, and you were to check in on him in 3-4 years, you'll see a vastly different operation. The computer store will still be his core business, but it will be barely recognizable.

He'll have an entire list of other business within his core business connected to it. Among them, he'll likely have some level of online sales and service, perhaps 2-3 specialized areas, each a revenue source. He'll have training classes designed specially for the savvy needs of young people (millennials). He'll also provide some kind of teachings and courses for the 55 and older niche. He'll have strategic alliances with other businesses that support his operation. He'll offer various levels of membership programs for his regular clients with up-sells and VIP options. He'll offer several informational products and courses, sold both online and offline. He'll likely have some kind of annual out-of-town events for his most elite clients. He may provide some kind of VIP trip to Google, Microsoft, or Apple, or similar online computer giants.

That's an entrepreneur.

By nature, and with our encouragement and direction, the true entrepreneur is constantly growing and diversifying. They can't stop manufacturing ideas. They can't stop thinking "entrepreneurial" outside the box. They refuse to leave any ideas in their head.

When you're an entrepreneur, you're *much* more than just a business owner.

Take Richard Branson for example. At the time of this writing, Branson, founder of Virgin Group, has more than 400 companies! Why on earth would he want to be involved in so many different businesses? It sure isn't because he needs the money. The simple answer: he's an entrepreneur.

The big breakthrough in your business is when you become an entrepreneur. When you keep trying to squeeze more out of the same business, there's only so much juice there to get.

There's a lot more juice to get out of a business with entrepreneurial strategies.

In a pet store in Boulder, CO or a dentist office in Ft. Lauderdale, FL, there's only so much revenue you can get from the core business. It's when you begin to think outside the box that things really begin to change. When you start thinking like an entrepreneur, you think in terms of expansion and diversification. You think vertical growth.

Uncovering The Hidden Gems Inside Your Business

Years ago when clients hired me, they typically needed a direct-response copywriter. They needed me to write good sales copy for them. Things are different now. Since those days, my business has morphed into a full-service marketing and consulting company. Nowadays when someone hires me, they realize I know far more about marketing than just writing a great sales campaign. They know they're working with a small business marketing consultant. We routinely uncover numerous revenue opportunities within their core business. In many cases, for less than they thought their investment would be.

From a marketing perspective, that's the way you should be thinking of your business.

A true entrepreneur thinks about their business differently than a typical business owner. They know their core business is just the tip of the iceberg. They never stop searching for offshoot opportunities. Savvy marketers know how to find these marketing gems. Often the big breakthrough occurs through consulting and collaboration.

Here's what I mean. For this example, let's say Person A works as a realtor. One day she decides she's had a belly full of working as an agent. She decides she wants to step up her game, take the leap, and become a real estate broker. She gets a loan, rents some office furniture, and bingo, she's up and running. As last, she's a broker. She continues to work hard for the next 25 years, eventually creating a very respectable and profitable business.

Great job.

Now, Person B does the same thing as Person A. She too decides she's had enough of being a realtor. She becomes a broker, except she doesn't stop there. This savvy broker has spent the last several years studying direct marketing. She sees the value of thinking beyond the normal confines of her business. She hires a marketing consulting company to help her with her marketing. She starts marketing her business in a way that leaves her competitors clueless. Soon she soon opens a property management division within her company. She sends out a monthly offline newsletter to her prospects and clients. Next she creates an Ambassador's Club for her most valued clients.

A year or two later, she opens a Home Watch Service for part-time residents and snowbirds. She opens a marketing and sales training center for real estate agents. Along the way, she authors several books, each promoting a division of her company, and her unique style of marketing. She grows her business vertically.

Do you see the difference?

This is not a make-believe business story. I just told you the story of one of our clients. Her name is Veronica Edwards. She's the proud broker/owner of Elite Real Estate and Property Management in Ormond Beach, FL. Veronica "gets it". She thinks like an entrepreneur, not a business owner.

I remember the day I opened the doors to my local marketing group in Daytona Beach. Veronica was one of the first people in the room. She was nervous, but didn't quit. She didn't know much about direct marketing back then, but always had a great attitude. And to this day, it's served her well. As busy as she was back then learning how to be a real estate broker, Veronica always made time to attend my meetings. Twice a month she was there like clockwork. Veronica's business continues to develop and expand vertically because she thinks like a marketer. Always working "on" her business, and not "in" it.

I can typically spot the struggling business owners who hear about our group. They drop by and kick our tires. A handful even comes back a second time. But, usually, like a fading sunset, most eventually disappear. The ironic part is, they're the ones who say they're too busy to attend but who need what we teach the most. The harsh reality is, the most successful business owners NEVER stop learning. They always have their ear to the rail, constantly learning the newest and most effective direct marketing strategies. They understand that school is NEVER out for the pro. As the saying goes, you're either growing or dying... you can't do both.

When you decide to be an entrepreneur, you must make a pact with yourself – a personal commitment to constantly raise the bar. Many people misunderstand the true meaning of an entrepreneur. Some see it as being greedy or overachieving. Instead they should be viewed as someone with a powerful vision. Where some see problems, the entrepreneur sees opportunity.

As an entrepreneur, your mindset is different. You never give up. You're like the cheerleader that's still screaming and yelling even though your team is behind by 46 points, and there's only 15 seconds left in the game.

My hope is that you'll be the entrepreneur who is never satisfied with status quo... the one with a vision for several opportunities wrapped around your core business.

CHAPTER 10
Turn Persistence Into Pay Dirt

Let's break out the old *Funk & Wagnalls* and look up the word "persistence".

As an adjective, persistence is defined as: "being persistent; especially in spite of all obstacles and distractions." As in, "a most persistent young man." It can also mean lasting and enduring. As in, "the persistent aroma of lavender." It's even been known to be constant or continued. As in, "such a persistent noise."

Passion, Patience, And Persistence: The Success Formula For Direct Response Marketing

Successful entrepreneurs and small business owners know how to be persistent without being annoying. They not only know how to regularly have something relevant, helpful, informative and entertaining to say, they know when to say it and how. They're not viewed as sales "pests".

Are you a pest or welcomed guest?

That question was first coined by Dan Kennedy way back in 1974. Yes, even in the pre-Internet, pre-social media days, when cold calling was the way most businesses operated, Kennedy explained that cold-call sales pushed people away while direct response marketing attracted them.

If you, or your sales force are still making cold calls, you're a pest! And the "pest" is becoming less and less welcome in the world of business commerce. The welcomed guest on the other hand, is what some call the "new" breed of salesperson.

Cold calling is for people who don't want to THINK and learn something new and different. As Henry Ford once said, "Thinking is the hardest thing there is. That's why almost no one does it."

The welcomed "guest", on the other hand, is just that – welcome. They're the ones who can help their prospects and clients solve a problem and add value and benefit to all involved. The welcome guest is persistent without irritating people with the rude, intrusive behavior of cold calling.

In today's small business marketing and advertising, you must have persistency in order to become more successful. Being in the game for the long haul has to be part of your marketing plan. You can't wake up one Tuesday morning and say, "I think I'll run an ad today."

That's the persistency I'm talking about. You can't decide, "Well, I'll try this a couple of times, and if it doesn't work, oh well."

If our clients don't have a set marketing and advertising budget, we strongly recommend they start one. No marketing and advertising campaign works without persistency, and it's hard to be persistent without a set budget.

Here's yet another story from my client files. We recently signed up a new client and got right to work on their first marketing and sales campaign. We produced a great, content-rich sales letter for them. It was being sent to a concentrated, well-qualified list of prospects. Our final draft approval meeting was great. The campaign was ready to rock n roll. As we said our good-byes, I mentioned to the client, "Okay, we'll be sending you the first draft for the 10-day follow-up letter in about 2 days."

There was an uncomfortable pause. It was as if the phone line went dead. I said, "Hello, are you there?" They finally answered with, "Follow-up letters?" They had no idea what we were talking about. This company was stuck in the old marketing mold. I told him, "Yes sir. The campaign isn't only a one-shot letter."

I went on to explain how there would be a follow-up letter every 10 days for 5 mailings to everyone who hadn't responded to previous mailings. Then a letter we like to refer to as a "Life Guard Letter," which lets prospects know you're there when needed. Then there's a final follow-up later with some finality in it.

You have to remain persistent with your marketing in a way that is pleasing to your target audience.

One of the most successful tools in our marketing toolbox that achieves persistence without being a pest is the newsletter. We talked about the newsletter in chapter 7.

Let's stay with our new client scenario. He is extremely impressed with the marketing strategy we laid out for him. He now fully understands where all this is going. He's prepared to start sending a monthly newsletter to the same hot prospects. Every month his newsletter will be on someone's desk at that prospect's business.

His newsletter is going to be exactly that. It will not be all about our client's business. It will contain articles about the prospect's field of interests. It may even have someone's grandmother's secret chocolate chip cookie recipe… something pleasing and rewarding with the prospect's best interest in mind. When you deliver friendly information like that, you're not the pest. You're the guest.

So many times it has very little to do with "what" you're marketing, but so much to do with "how" you market.

Using the right tools, targeting the right audience, and

being in it for the long haul... that's the way you turn persistence into pay dirt.

CHAPTER 11
Collaboration & Masterminds

The President of the United States of America has a cabinet full of executives to assist him in guiding the nation. The largest, most profitable companies in the world have a board of directors advising the CEO on which course of action he or she should take in order to remain profitable. Even the world's top athletes have coaches and trainers in order to keep them at the top of their game.

Allow me to clarify something with you. You may be a self-employed owner or have one or two employees. Or you could have a much bigger operation. Even though you may feel alone and on your own, rest assured your feelings and challenges are not unique. Business owners of every size deal with similar issues.

Let me give you an example of what I mean.

A few years ago I wrote a series of marketing campaigns for an association comprised of owners and CEOs from small to medium sized companies all over the country. It was interesting to discover that the challenges with these CEOs were exactly the same as the solopreneur. Bottom line, we're all members of the same club.

The good news is… you *own* your own business. The bad news is… you *own* your own business. It's a double-edged sword for sure.

Success is rarely a singular event. Truly successful business owners will seek out and collaborate with other owners. They'll join something called a mastermind group.

If you're familiar with Napoleon Hill's business classic, *Think And Grow Rich*, you'll be familiar with the concept of a mastermind group. Hill's book recounts how many successful business people rely on a small, tight-knit group of advisors to help them build their businesses.

I've long been an advocate of assembling some form of entrepreneurs and small business owners to help you grow your business. The right mastermind group can provide numerous benefits. Mastermind groups give you a chance to get feedback from others who have no dog in your fight. They'll help you fix problems and improve what's working for you.

Truth is, it's damn hard to spot problems in your own business. You're just too close to the action. You need like-minded people to collaborate with. And in the business world, a mastermind group is hands down THE best way to solve that problem.

Without outside help, you tend to get consumed by your day-to-day routines and wind up feeling like the Lone Ranger. You end up running in circles chasing work, looking for new business, with no navigational compass. That's no way to run a business.

Everyone can use a few marketing *compadres* to bounce ideas off of. Without a good sounding board, your best ideas might often stay on the cutting room floor. Or worse, they never get developed.

I learned this lesson the hard way several years ago. At the time, I thought I had a pretty good handle on my marketing. Looking back, I learned some valuable lessons that could have been avoided had there been someone in my camp to solve my marketing problems sooner. It would have saved me a lot of time and money.

At the time, I knew nothing about mastermind groups. I

do now. And now, after reading this book, you will too. Knowing what you know now, let me ask you a question...

Who's Got Your Back?

Sometimes, when I meet a fellow business owner, I'll ask them, "Who's looking out for you while you're searching for creative ways to grow your business? Who's your sounding board?"

Most people struggle with their answer. Even seasoned veterans tend to wiggle around for a good answer. Others don't respond at all. Instead, they give me a glassy stare. The deer in the headlights look. For most, my question is the nudge they need to realize they've been going about it all wrong.

Steven Covey, author of *The 7 Habits Of Highly Effective People*, refers to the process as "sharpening your saw." Covey uses the analogy of the woodcutter who works like a dog, sweating, straining, and putting in long, hard days with a dull blade.

Don't be the woodcutter. Stop and sharpen your blade. Find a marketing mastermind group in your area and join it.

Earlier in this book, I mentioned that twice a month I host a 2-hour mentoring session on marketing and advertising. The meetings take place at the University of Central Florida's Business Incubator in Daytona Beach, Florida.

Sessions have between 5-10 business owners on hand. Once the ideas start flowing, wheels start turning. Engines start humming, and the energy becomes contagious. Brainstorming officially begins to kick in. Smartphone "record" buttons get pushed and copious notes are taken.

People leave our mastermind event with real solutions to their marketing challenges. The mentoring sessions are also what I refer to as "brain dump" sessions.

This is true collaboration. It doesn't matter if people are in the same industry or not. The gray matter gets to jelling and ideas start flowing. Attendees can't wait to talk about their businesses. They're proud of what they created; they're ready to shout about it from the rooftops.

I chair two mastermind groups. In addition, I'm also member of two other marketing groups. One group is in Orlando, the other in Houston. Now, you may be thinking... hmmmm, "Texas? That's a long way from Florida." You might be surprised to know that, regardless of where you are geographically, our problems and challenges are the same.

If this is your first exposure to mastermind groups, let me forewarn you. There are free groups, and there are groups that charge. From my personal experience, as in most things in life, you tend to get what you pay for. You'll always feel more vested when you have a little skin in the game.

Do some research. Check out the site MeetUp.com. Check out the various marketing meetings in your area. Chances are you'll find one or more in your city or town. Make arrangements to attend a local event. Give it a try. If you find one you don't like, don't give up. Keep searching until you find a group that meets the criteria you're looking for.

If you happen to be in the Central Florida area, reach out to me. My email is: RodHarter@me.com. I'm happy to give you some direction or share the details of our local mastermind groups. As a participant, you'll get equal time in our hot seat. That's when we give you the floor, and the rest of the group will focus on your business. We'll help you solve your biggest marketing challenges.

CHAPTER 12
Become An Author

As you know, it's highly competitive out there, probably more so than ever before. In order to stand out, your business needs a secret weapon that puts it head and shoulders above your competitors. If anything depends on your success, it's your ability to open doors.

You're surrounded by competitors, each of you fighting for the same customers. It's not as easy as it used to be, to bring people in the front door to do business with you. Along the way you've probably taken your stab at different marketing and advertising strategies. And, for the most part, none of them brought in the amount of new business you hoped for.

How many times have you said you'd do whatever it took to find an effective, inexpensive way to attract a steady flow of new business without having to start from square one every month? A book is that one big thing to get you over that hump.

Well, I have the answer. Write a book.

Yes, your own, authored book. Now, before you tighten up and feel like a book is out of the question, stick with me a moment. We'll get to the nuts and bolts of creating your own book in a minute. First, I want to open your eyes to just how impactful a book will be to your business from an advertising and marketing standpoint.

NOTHING quite matches the prestige and professionalism as the moment you take a book out of your briefcase, slide it across a desk, and give it to a prospect. Or, when you use a book as a powerful lead generation tool to attract prospects to your website. A book places you in a class by yourself.

Having your own book is a game changer, and to clarify, I'm not talking about a book you sell on Amazon. You can put your book on Amazon and may sell a few copies, but you won't make much money. Trying to make money "selling" a book these days is a bad idea. You heard me right. Even veteran authors have a hard time making any money selling books these days. The margins are very slim, and you'd have to sell tens of thousands of copies to make any money. Bottom line, it's not likely to happen.

I'm referring to a book that you self-publish and use as a powerful lead generation tool. With the right strategies, having your own, authored book will create numerous revenue opportunities for you. For starters, you can use a book for:

- Lead generation
- Speaking engagements
- Self-promotion (without having to "sell")
- Powerful referral opportunities
- Attracting prospects to your website(s)
- Radio/TV/Newspaper interviews and articles
- Recognition as an expert in your market
- Celebrity status
- Business alliances
- And much more

Having your own book is the great equalizer. It will bring you business and open doors, even if you compete with much bigger companies. You'll be seen as a published author... the consummate expert in your field.

Compare a book to any other marketing tool, and it's not

even close. The prestige and recognition of becoming a published author is unmatched.

You'll be known in your market like a local celebrity. The benefits are endless.

Think about how differently your prospects and clients will view and treat you. You'll get more new business because you'll be the logical choice for people looking for what you sell!

Once you discover the many ways to promote and market your book, you'll begin to attract new business. You'll also get more respect from those who do business with you because they'll view you as an expert. Not to mention, how your competitors will treat you when they interact with you.

Think of the impact a book will have on your clients. Do you think they'll be more likely to tell their friends and colleagues about you when you hand them a free, signed copy of your book?

I do.

You'll get free publicity (and all the new business that comes from it) from local newspapers and radio stations. The media is always looking for experts to interview, especially local published authors! Just think of the PR value of just one article written about you in your market... or one radio interview about your book or business. The additional free exposure can easily be worth an entire year's worth of paid advertising!

Think of the pride your clients will have when they tell their family and friends they use a semi-famous business owner.

Your existing customers will stay with you longer because they'll believe in your guidance and knowledge.

How To Get Your Book Written And Published

Now that I have your attention about how powerful a book can be for your business, let's talk about how to make it happen.

First and foremost, let me dispel a few myths about authoring your own book.

Myth #1: You have to be a great writer. Actually, you don't. In fact, if you can talk, you can write a book. I'll cover more on this in a moment.

Myth #2: Self-publishing will break the bank. Actually, writing, editing, and distributing your own book doesn't have to cost a fortune. Far from it. The return on your investment will probably startle you.

The whole book-writing landscape has changed. Technology has made writing your own book much easier and far more affordable than in the past. Today you can write your own book and have it self-published at a fraction of the price from just a few years ago. You can write it yourself or have someone ghostwrite it for you. More on this in a minute.

The best part is you can have as many or as few copies printed as you'd like. Gone are the days of having to pay upfront costs for 10,000 books that sit in your garage. All that has changed. Thanks to the world of self-publishing, you print your books on demand as your marketing needs dictate.

Got a special promotion or trade-show coming up and need 75 books? Easy enough. Just pick up the phone and place your order. In most cases, your books will be mailed to your door in 2-3 weeks. How's that for serious marketing? Talk about having an advantage over your competition.

And, as far as the book writing process goes, you don't need to burn the midnight oil for months or years. Gone are the days of having to write a 250-page book. Actually shorter, 75-85 page books work just fine. You'll accomplish the same thing faster and for less money. Think about that for a minute. How many books could you eventually have, each one promoting a specific product or service within your business?

For example, one of my clients and fellow mastermind members is Larry Weinstein. Larry is a CPA *and* a tax resolution specialist in Houston, TX. Larry helps clients with IRS problems, often when bankruptcy is not an option. As of this writing, Larry has authored 12 books, many of them less than 75 pages. Larry has established himself as "*the*" expert in his niche.

You can do the same thing for your business.

My point is this. We're all wired the same way. Your prospects and clients want to do business with someone who rises above the clutter. They want to do business with YOU, not your business. So, oblige them. Give them what they're desperately seeking – YOU. What better way to make that happen than with a book?

When someone runs across your website, sees one of your ads, or meets you in person, the first thing they think is, "Of all my choices for this product or service, why should I choose this person?" They want to know what makes YOUR business better and different than all their other choices.

If you don't have a good answer for this question, you have very little chance of moving the conversation forward. At this point, you're just another salesperson trying to pitch your goods and services.

Having your own book will change the dynamics of this process dramatically.

If you stop and think about it, every business you compete

with has fancy brochures, business cards, and websites. However, when you offer a book as a lead generation tool or give it to someone, you're showing up like nobody else.

Here's the deal. Until you give your prospects a reason why YOUR business is different than your competitors, they'll continue to lump you into the same category with everybody else. YOU know you're better – but they don't. So, it's your job to show them you're better. Failure to "wow" them at this point, and they'll instantly deem you as a commodity.

Show your prospects you're the obvious choice. Give them a book that's jam-packed with valuable information.

Start with an attention-getting story. Your "hook".

Your bio can be next, followed by information you want your prospects to know about your business, the "nuts and bolts" of your product and/or services. Share the kind of information your prospects can't get anywhere else. The key is to make sure your book is personal and conversational, written in your voice. It should be easy to read, so people can skim through it and still get great value. Use short sentences and paragraphs. Use bullets and lists for easy reference as much as possible.

Truth is, most people won't read your book cover to cover. That's okay. By the time someone's holding your book in their hands, you've already accomplished your biggest goal. As they affix their eyes on the front and back cover, they'll say to themselves, "Damn, this person's a published author? Wow! Very impressive. They're undoubtedly 'the' expert on this subject."

Your book will quickly boost your credibility. You see, society has always put published authors on a pedestal. We hold authors in high esteem. Those you give your book to will feel honored and amazed at your knowledge and expertise. They'll feel a special bond with you… a unique level of trust, rapport, and credibility.

So, the big question is …

What If You're Not A Writer

I have some good news for you. You don't have to be a good writer anymore. In fact, you don't have to be a writer at all. If you can talk, you can write a book. You can even have your book ghostwritten.

There are plenty of resources on the Internet to help you write your book. A couple of the more popular ones are www.guru.com and www.upwork.com. I use both of these resources for outsourcing projects all the time. There are also plenty of other writing resources on the Internet with a full spectrum of pricing options. Again, keep in mind, when it comes to the Internet, you're likely going to get what you pay for. I wouldn't suggest you try to cut corners on a book. It's too important to promote a book on a shoestring budget.

Once in a while, depending on my schedule, I'll take on a book project for a client. I let my clients tell their story to me.

It's funny because for many people, the thought of "talking their story" tightens them up. They'll say, "Rod, I haven't a clue how to tell my story." That's the beauty of my system. You don't need to worry about any of that. If we ended up working on a project together, we wouldn't necessarily start at the beginning. We'd start by having a couple of friendly, one-on-one conversations together. The editing part is done later. At the beginning, it's about priming the pump, asking you thought-provoking questions about your business, your family, your likes, your dislikes, etc. We'll cover information your readers won't hear anywhere else. Once you get rolling, your natural passion for your business will take over. It happens with every client. At some point, you'll forget the call is even being recorded. This is critical because that's the precise moment you begin to hit your sweet spot. Once you find your groove, the conversation begins to naturally flow. It's much easier to do than you think. If you stop and think about it, who knows more about your business than you?

We might have a total of 2-3 calls together. Once the calls are done, your part is over. That's when the writing and editing part begins. I'll listen to our calls a few times, carefully listening for your hook and other interesting parts of your story. It doesn't take a lot of conversation to fill a 75-100-page book.

You can spend $10K... 20K... 30K on a self-published book – but you don't have to. You can get a book done for a fraction of those prices. And, depending on your product or service price point, just 1-2 leads from your book can offset your initial investment. Everything after that is pure gravy.

You can have your book cover designed for as little as $15 on www.fiverr.com. A word of caution here – again, you'll likely get what you pay for. Consider spending a little more money and get a professionally designed book cover. There's no benefit to packaging your transcripts around a cheesy-looking book cover. That's like buying a Steinway piano, and only knowing how to play "Chopsticks."

If you'd like to know more about working on a book project together, email me at **RodHarter@me.com** and we'll set up a consultation appointment together.

More Ways To Promote Your Book

Another huge benefit to having your own book is using it as a lead generation tool.

The sky's the limit here.

You can also create short audios or videos. Some people are readers, some are listeners, others like to get their information from videos. Offer all three as lead-generation tools.

When your book is completed, you'll have in your possession one of the most powerful lead-generation tools you could ever have. This is particularly useful if you're in a profession with restrictions on how you advertise and the use of client testimonials. A book can be used to draw attention to your business without actually advertising it. In other words, in many situations you can promote your book and not your business. Use your book as a lead-generation tool. It will help you gain notoriety and celebrity status.

Marketed properly, your book will take you right to the top of your class, even in a market saturated with competition. There are plenty of creative ways to market and promote your book. For example, you can use simple, self-standing website landing pages to collect email addresses so you can continue your dialog with prospects. You can give your book away, or charge a small handling fee to cover postage. The opportunities are unlimited.

For example, let's say you're an insurance company and compete with 50 other companies in your local market. The only difference is, you have a book on the subject AND a lead-generation marketing system that attracts qualified leads to your business 24/7. All things being equal, whom do you think a prospect would be more inclined to engage with? An insurance agent with a business card, or one who's "written the book" on the subject and hands it to their client? It's an easy answer, don't you think? A book will trump everything else hands down – every time.

The Big Money Is In Your List

Ask any successful marketer and they'll tell you the secret

to rapid growth is "their list." And the best part is, you don't have to figure this out on your own. I've always felt it's much easier (and wiser) to observe those who have already accomplished what you'd like to do, and do what they've done. You don't have to start with a blank canvas. Success leaves clues. Find yourself someone who's blazed a path of success in your niche and pay close attention to them.

Top marketers in every industry follow a few basic direct marketing rules. They know the money is in their list. Refer to the guidelines in Chapter 6 about lead generation.

Produce something of value for your prospects and give it to them for free. Your goal is to get their email. When a prospect opts-in to get your "freemium", an exchange is made. Give them what they want, and they give you... their email. Email addresses are added to software programs called auto-responders. Auto-responders are powerful tools, and very few of your competitors (if any) use them. There are many of these types of email services on the Internet. I use AWeber (www.AWeber.com) for my business, at $19 month, with no long-term contract.

For the most part, auto-responders are totally automated. Set up the software once, and it will communicate with your prospect list around the clock. You basically set it, and forget it. Email messages are then distributed at a pre-determined frequency to your list. With the click of a button, your prospects can forward their emails to friends, neighbors, and colleagues.

Any of these marketing strategies are effective on their own. However, when combined with your own, authored book – watch out! You'll have at your fingertips a very powerful marketing SYSTEM. Best of all, your competitors won't have a clue how to compete with you.

More Options To Support Your Book

Create a series of short audio interviews. Have someone ask you frequently asked questions about your products and/or services. Audios can be offered as a single downloadable MP3 or broken up into shorter clips. They can be listened to on a smartphone, tablet or computer.

Pull back the curtain and share advice your competitors aren't giving your prospects. You'll quickly separate yourself from the pack and be seen as much more than just another widget maker. Instead of being viewed as a pesky salesperson, you'll be looked at as a trusted advisor… someone who is there to solve your prospect's problems. Selling will soon be replaced with trust.

A well-constructed, lead generation system virtually eliminates the need to do cold call prospecting or hard selling. Your prospects will begin to qualify and "close" themselves. They'll view you as a leader in your niche… a problem solver. You'll do less selling and more educating. You'll create the most value as the obvious choice for their business.

CHAPTER 13
The Podcast

Back in Chapter 7, "Newsletter Magic", we covered the numerous benefits of publishing your own newsletter. Its similarity to a newspaper allows us to take some liberties, and consider it one of the many mediums used, to get the word out to your prospects and clients.

Radio carried that same clout when it was first introduced. Radio ruled the airwaves for many generations. Then, along came television. Radio's popularity waned, and it slowly became the "stepchild" of the broadcast mediums.

Good news. The concept of radio is working its way back onto the charts. It doesn't take millions of dollars for plush studios, broadcasting equipment, licensing or hiring high priced talent. It's called "podcasting", and it can be done right in the comfort of your own business or home.

The term podcast was first mentioned by Ben Hammersly in an article in the February 2004 edition of the *Guardian* newspaper. Due to the huge popularity of the iPod, they coined the term as a reference. They used the name "iPod" as a broadcasting tool to promote podcasts.

The "podcast" was born.

There are quite a few advantages that podcasts have over radio shows. Podcasts are extremely user friendly and convenient. They can be listened to anytime, anywhere, by anyone. They are broadcast over the Internet and heard on any device that receives the Internet. In today's technology, that's virtually anywhere in the world.

An edition of the *Merriam Webster* dictionary defines "podcast" as a program of either music or talk available in a digital format for automatically downloading over the Internet.

It has some of the decision makers in radio thinking twice about their established practices and preconceptions about audiences, consumption, production, and distribution. To them, the podcast is seen as somewhat disruptive, due largely to the facts that no "one" person owns the technology, it's completely free to listen to, and its content is up to the creator. All of these facts are a complete departure from the traditional model of "gate kept" media. Consumers become producers, producers become consumers, and they engage one another.

The audio or video file associated with any podcast in a series is maintained by a central distributor's web feed. I use Libsyn as my distributor. I produce the podcast, download it to Libsyn, establish the release time and date, then select which venues Libsyn should distribute to. In my case, my podcast can be heard on iTunes and Stitcher Radio. Libsyn provides usage, download, and listener reports. I get feedback on which shows are hitting the market and which shows are less attractive. It's an amazing tool to massage and fine-tune your productions.

Podcasting was once an obscure, hardly known method of spreading information. Today it's a popular, recognized medium for distributing content on either a corporate or personal level. Listeners also have the opportunity to be selective to what shows they want to hear and when they want to hear them.

According to a statistic released in April 2015 by Pew Research Center, "The percentage of Americans who have listened to a podcast in the past month has almost doubled since 2008, from 9% to 17% by January of 2015. In the first half of 2015, the percentage of listeners is already up two points over the same period in 2014."

Edison Research also reported that one-third (33%) of all Americans 12 years of age or older now say they have listened to at least one podcast. It's no wonder the radio executives are worried. Their competition's audience is growing steadily. Podcasts are not only becoming more popular each year, they are definitely here to stay. This is why you should be considering producing and distributing your own podcast.

Every major automobile manufacturer now offers models that support Apple's versions of iTunes, or is planning to introduce it soon.

In January 2016, Apple released a complete list of car models that now natively support the use of its CarPlay (iPhone mirroring interface.)

Apple's list of CarPlay-enabled vehicles includes over a hundred 2016 and 2017 models from 21 auto manufacturers. CarPlay allows users to replicate their iPhone's look and capabilities on a car's central console through the use of hands-free and eyes-free access to Apple Maps, phone, messages, iTunes and many third-party apps such as iHeartRadio and Spotify.

It was this announcement by Apple last year that first got my attention. I was excited about the prospects of having my podcast played in all these 2016 car models and beyond. I figured if Apple was making this big of a commitment, I wanted to be a part of it.

I released my first podcast, *Marketing You Can Do Right Now,* May 19, 2015. I had 42 downloads after that first show. Barely three months later, by the end of July, I had over 2,700 downloads. The popularity of the podcast has enabled me to market and advertise to a "worldwide audience". That's something I know my marketing and advertising budget would have never been able to accomplish.

That's right… *my* marketing and advertising budget. I practice what I preach. I have a budget for my marketing. As my business grows, so does my budget. Podcasting has provided an avenue of amazing exposure for a fraction of the cost. Now with podcasting, my show can be heard from Kalamazoo and Kathmandu, and any point in between.

At the time of this writing, I've had my podcast on the air about 10 months. I often interview experts from various areas of direct marketing. I also have a handful of regular contributors on my show. None of it is scripted. I've tried it both ways, and for me, things feel fresher when it's not scripted or rehearsed.

It's been something I've rather enjoyed.

"Gee Rod, this all sounds great, but I'll bet it's expensive and time consuming."

Great point. I'm glad you brought it up. Yes. It can be expensive, and yes, it can be time consuming. However, you'd be surprised to find out how many podcasters got their start by simply talking into their phone's recording device and still do that today. On the other hand, there are podcasters who've set up elaborate studios with state-of-the-art recording equipment, elaborate background music, and guest speakers.

That's all part of the beauty of podcasting. You make it what you want it to be. Remember, you're doing this to grow your business. Sometimes you can get carried away, and suddenly you're a show producer first and a business owner second. It's that contagious.

So how do you get started? You must first determine two important points. Point number one: do you have the written material and subject matter to produce a captivating and interesting podcast on a regular basis? Remember the chapter on turning features into benefits? You have to be producing something your listeners find valuable. I've heard podcasts that were so full of great information I listened to them two or three times. I've also heard podcasts that put me to sleep in a minute and a half. If you can't keep your listeners interested, don't bother with a podcast. Save your time and money.

Point number two: are you ready to produce your shows on a regular basis? In addition to producing a 20-30 minute podcast every week, I also produce two 'Marketing Minutes' that run 4-6 minutes each week. Think about your morning drive radio show. It's there for you every Monday through Friday at 7:00 a.m. If you're a Sunday morning news junkie like me, *Meet The Press* is there for you every Sunday morning. Your podcast must become a regular feature for your listeners. You can't see them, but they're out there, and once they like you, they'll want to hear you early and often.

Recall what I said earlier. Your listeners aren't restricted to morning drive times or a scheduled broadcast on a specific day of the week. They can listen to you on *their* schedule. Make sure they have something new and refreshing each podcast. If you can't produce your shows on a regular basis, save your time and money. A podcast isn't for you.

Don't misunderstand what I'm saying here. I know I sound like "Debbie Downer" all of a sudden, but I'm giving it to you straight. Producing podcasts aren't easy to do. They take a lot of time, effort, and preparation.

When I was doing my research, I listened to a lot of podcasts on the subject. People made it sound like it was so easy. They said, "Just sit down, close your door, and put in a few hours of work. The next thing you know, you're up and running."

It didn't work that way for me.

There are plenty of online courses on the Internet, in every price range, many taught by superstar podcasters. If you have the time and money, this might be a good option for you to help you get started.

Here are two popular podcast resources I found to be very credible:

www.podcastanswerman.com by Cliff Ravenscraft
www.eofire.com by John Lee Dumas

I'm not affiliated with either one of these gentlemen, nor am I being compensated by them in any way. I listened to a lot of their information and downloaded some of their reports.

Podcast production is not something you have to do on your own. Some of our clients sub-contract the production of their podcasts. Either way, they work, and they're here to stay.

Here are my humble beginnings as a podcaster. I bought a quality headset/microphone. I paid about $40 for it. Prices can vary. They can be as cheap as $10, but I wanted a professional, quality sound, so I went with the higher quality model.

I first opened a podcast account on iTunes and Stitcher Radio. There are other venues, but as of this writing, these are the two biggest platforms.

Next, I established an account with Skype and Libsyn. I use Skype as a two-fold tool. It not only allows me to record my conversation, but I can have a cohost or guest join me as well. I send them a password and they join me on my Skype account. We speak for typically 25-30 minutes on our topic. At this point, I forward the show to my editing department. I like editing the shows myself. When I'm too busy, I outsource it.

After the editing process is done, I upload the show to Libsyn. Libsyn uploads it to iTunes and Stitcher Radio. Next thing you know, bingo, I'm a podcaster, and you can be too. If you're producing the right material, you'll begin to develop a following.

So what's a good download podcast number? According

to Rob Walch, VP of Podcaster Relations at Libsyn.com (the largest podcast media hosting company), in September 2013, a podcast episode that has been live approximately 30 days averages 141 downloads. If you have over 3,400 downloads, you are in the top 10%. If you have over 9,000 downloads, you are in the top 5%. Lastly, if you have over 50,000 downloads per episode (again after having it live for 30 days), you are in the top 1%. This would be the Marc Marons, Adam Corrolas, Jay Mohrs, etc, of the podcasting world. Marc Maron has even spawned his own TV show on the IFC cable channel from his podcast.

Podcasting is a very powerful marketing tool. It's something you should consider for your business.

CHAPTER 14
Mind Management & Goal Setting

Hopefully as you've read this book, you've been taking notes… maybe even highlighted a few pages along the way and are getting your creative juices flowing.

Next, take the momentum and knowledge you've gained and start working on a marketing plan, both mentally and physically.

Before you start, allow me to share a few basic facts to help with your plan. <u>There are only three ways to increase your business</u>:

- Increase the number of clients you have
- Increase the average size of the sale, per client
- Increase the number of times clients return and buy from you again

That's it. Those are the three areas you must focus on. Things will get easier once you break the process down into simple, manageable, action steps.

If all this is new to you, it's okay. Take a few deep breaths. Ease into it.

Here's why. Your inner consciousness is a powerful force. Its influence is felt in every aspect of your life. It is, in fact, the most important part of who you are and the main reason for your success or failure.

When you apply your mental mindset to your business,

there's a right way to *think* about this process.

"Hope" Is A Terrible Business Strategy

Just wanting something badly won't make it happen. Hoping for something different to happen won't work either. Even working long hours every day is not enough. Your business will always remain where it is – until you change your thinking. It's true in business, as it is in life.

Ideally, you want to strengthen your mind the same way you'd condition other muscles in your body. Just like learning how to ballroom dance, playing a musical instrument, or speaking another language… anything you want to get good at will take time.

We're not going to delve deep into the human mind in this book. However, I do believe it's worth having a general understanding of how your mind works. If you'd like to learn more about this subject, I recommend you pick up a couple of books. One is *The Power Of Your Subconscious Mind* by Dr. Joseph Murphy. The other is *Mind Power Into The 21st Century* by John Kehoe. Both are inspiring reads and international bestsellers.

In a nutshell, here's how your mind works. The ideas and thoughts you accept as true in your conscious mind, are accepted by your subconscious mind. Your subconscious does not know the difference between good and bad, big and small, up or down. This is what makes it so powerful.

Think of your subconscious as fertile soil that will nourish any seed (conscious thoughts) you put into it. Just as the soil doesn't care whether you plant the seed of a rose, an apple tree or a weed, the subconscious mind does not care if you "seed" thoughts that are good or bad. It will nourish all of them equally and eventually bring them into your life experiences.

What's all this "mind talk" got to do with your business? Plenty. When your mindset is channeled and focused, you'll approach your marketing with far greater clarity. It's another reason why you should be thinking about marketing every day. It's not something you can tinker around with once in a while or when business is down.

You Get Good At What You Focus On

Here's what I mean. When we were in school, we learned our timetables. If I were to ask you what's 7 x 7, you'd know immediately it's 49. If I asked you what's 8 x 10, you know it's 80. How do you know those things? It's because they've been imprinted in your mind a countless number of times, over and over and over again. Yet, if I were to ask you what 13 x 8 was, you wouldn't know, or at least not as quickly, because we were only taught multiplication tables up to 12.

Our multiplication tables are imprinted deep into our consciousness. The same thing is true with our language. It too has been imprinted into our consciousness. It's the reason you can read this book and understand the words. Our vocabulary has been imprinted into our consciousness. These are two examples of "imprinting" that have happened in our life.

Imprint "Empowering Beliefs" Deep Into Your Mind

The third and most fascinating, challenging, and interesting imprinting, is to imprint empowering beliefs into your consciousness.

You do this the same way as with the multiplication tables. **You focus on beliefs you choose to believe.**

Every evening before you go to bed, take five minutes to think about the power of your mind, about the power of choice, and how you can choose your thoughts… and how thoughts have power to them. By choosing your thoughts, you can direct and influence your actions. You can create energy within you that will attract realities to you. This is very powerful.

Spend five minutes every day contemplating this, thinking about it, affirming to yourself that you have unlimited power. At first, sometimes you might get really excited. You will come out of your short exercise empowered. Other times, it will feel like you're lying to yourself. Your mind might say, "Who are you kidding… you don't have unlimited power." Sometimes the exercise will feel cold and mechanical. Other times it will feel exciting and empowering. The key is to do it every day.

Chart yourself. Don't miss a day. Whether it's exciting or boring, don't stop. Do it every day. Mind power needs repetition. Somewhere between 60 and 90 days, somewhere around this period, you will wake up with this reality that you have unlimited power at your disposal. You'll know it. You'll feel it. And from that point on, you'll never doubt it, much the same way you never doubted 7 x 7 was 49. Just make sure you make this a small part of your day, every day.

Repetition is the key with mind power. It's the difference between just positive thinking and mind power.

Take Action

The fact that you've read this far tells me you're ready to make serious changes to your business. That process starts with having a few specific business goals. We're not going to go too in depth with goal setting in this book, but I do want to get you moving in the right direction.

Organize your thoughts and start working on an action plan. As the old adage goes, action beats meditation every time.

Whenever I host a marketing group, I'll often ask how

many people believe in the power of having written goals. Every hand shoots up. Yet, when I ask how many of them have written goals, almost every hand goes down.

You may have tried goal setting in the past. Maybe it didn't work for you, or you didn't see immediate results and gave up on it. It's understandable. I've done the same thing.

All that changed for me 17 years ago when I began taking the advice from the most creative minds in the area of small business marketing and having a stronger 'mental mindset'. It takes focus to stay on track. There are distractions everywhere at every turn. However, just like making time for your kids or the gym, you've got to reserve time for yourself.

Find a quiet place in your home or office. Take a little time to focus on your business. Think of one or two things that if implemented over the next 7… 30… 60 days, would have the biggest impact on your business.

Now think a little longer term. Where would you like to see your business a year… two years… five years from now? What will your business look like? Be careful not to restrict yourself. Think about what Napoleon Hill said in his classic business book, *Think And Grow Rich*, "Whatever the mind can conceive, it can achieve." Allow your thoughts to be the fuel for your imagination. Be sure to remove any constraints, as if money were not an issue.

Be Goal Oriented

Experts on the science of success know the brain is a goal-seeking organism. Whatever goal you give to your subconscious mind, it will work constantly to achieve.

One of the best ways to get clarity and specificity on your goals is to **write them out in detail**, as if you were writing details for a work order. Come up with some goals that will stretch you, but not to the point you can't accomplish them.

Your goals must meet certain criteria. They must identify exactly what you want to accomplish. Provide as much specificity as you can come up with. For example:

Bad goal: I want a new website.
Good goal: I am going to have a user-friendly, 9-page Wordpress site with personality and warmth. My site will have a lead-generation system, a series of audios and videos. Do you see the difference?

Your goals should be measurable. As the saying goes, "You can't manage what you can't measure." If possible, try to quantify the result. You want to know absolutely, positively whether or not you hit your goal.

Bad goal: Earn more this year than last.
Good goal: Earn $45,000 more this year than last.

Actionable – **every goal should start with an action verb** (quit, run, finish, eliminate, etc.) rather than a to-be verb (am, be, have, etc.)

Every goal needs a date associated with it. By that I mean, a date when you plan to deliver on that goal. It could be by year-end (December 31) or more near-term (September 30). A goal without a date, is just a dream. Make sure that every goal ends with a "by when" date.

Bad goal: Lose 15 pounds.
Good goal: Lose 15 pounds by December 31st.

Write your goals down. This is critical. There is huge power in writing your goals down, even if you never develop an action plan or do anything else (not recommended). When you write something down, you are stating your intention and setting things in motion.

Review your goals frequently. While writing your goals down is a powerful exercise in itself, the real juice is in reviewing them on a regular basis. This is what turns them into reality. Every time I review my goals, I ask myself, "What's the next step I need to take to move toward this goal?" I recommend you review your goals daily or weekly. I review mine every day. The key is to let your goals inspire you.

Find out what works best for you. Write them in a journal, use mind maps, vision boards, or whatever works for you. I like to use 3 x 5 cards. I describe every goal in great detail. I keep my cards on the nightstand next to my bed. When I get up in the morning, I spend a few minutes reviewing them. I do the same thing at night. When you assign your subconscious mind a project before you go to sleep, it will find a way to make that assignment happen. Your subconscious mind won't argue or dispute your goals. It doesn't know the difference between something you want or already have. It only knows what it constantly thinks about, good or bad.

Keep your goals to yourself, except with someone who is committed to helping you achieve them (your mentor, mastermind group, or business consultant).

The practice of goal setting is not just helpful, it's a prerequisite for happiness. Psychologists tell us that people who make consistent progress toward meaningful goals live happier, more satisfied lives than those who don't.

Goal setting will create a dramatic shift in your business and help you implement all the marketing strategies covered in this book. Once you've made a list of your goals, refer to them daily. Look at your list. Use it as your marketing guidance system. Doing so will keep you more focused and on target.

If you're ready to take goal setting to a higher level, I recommend you read *Maximum Achievement* by Brian Tracy. He's one of the all-time great motivators and business coaches. He covers goal setting at an almost scientific level.

Ask almost any successful person how they did it, and chances are they relied heavily on making goals a major part of their success blueprint.

You can't get to your destination without a roadmap. You need a mental compass. The goal is to transfer your creative thoughts into an actionable, marketing plan.

Don't try to do everything at once like the guy who decides he wants to suddenly get in shape, and spends the entire day in the gym. When he doesn't see instant results, he gets discouraged, and gives up. Don't be that guy.

Give yourself permission to think beyond normal boundaries.

Use this book as a reference tool for ideas. Figure out where your business is leaking oil. Look for opportunities you're not taking advantage of. Then set goals to address those issues and opportunities.

CHAPTER 15
Being "In It" For The Long Haul

I may have mentioned this once or twice already. No matter what style of marketing and advertising you use, it has to be a fixed-budget item. It must be something that is done on such a regular basis that it becomes second nature to you. If someone comes up to you and says, "Do you market and advertise?" Your answer must be, "My business wouldn't survive without it."

Here's a scenario that is all too familiar with today's small business owner.

Their marketing and advertising is basically a three-pronged campaign. They have a website, an eighth of a page in the yellow pages, and business cards. That's it. There's not even a budget to replace the business cards or renew the ad in the yellow pages. They just wait for the bill and hope there's enough in the bank to pay for it.

It is imperative to understand the importance of *consistency* in your marketing and advertising. Without mentioning any names, think about the world's largest producer of a product. Pick any product you wish. Now... imagine if that product never ran another commercial or ad again. It would drop off the face of the earth and disappear from shelves within a year.

In 2013 the largest soft drink manufacturer in the world, the Coca Cola Company, spent 3.7 billion dollars on marketing and advertising. 3.7 billion represents roughly 7% of the company's total gross revenue. Coke has said that advertising is a key strategy for their company's growth and success.

Between 2009 and 2013, quite a few companies have broached billion-dollar-a-year marketing and advertising budgets: Apple, Hewlett Packard, and Microsoft. But the Granddaddy of them all is Samsung. In 2013 Samsung spent a whopping 4.2 billion dollars on marketing and advertising. These are some seriously committed business people.

That list must include you and your business.

I too am a small businessman. I know full well I'll never see budgets like the ones we just went over. However, that doesn't mean I can't market and advertise. There are ways to make your dollars go further and do more.

The big boys may have huge pockets and be able to cast a net over a huge audience, but you have something they don't. You can make your message personal. You can "target" an audience. You can make your ads read as though they were written just for that set of eyes that's reading it right then.

You get the opportunity to build a rapport and relationships with your prospects. You're the local "go-to" person. People like dealing with people they know and trust. Big companies can only do that with discounts, giveaways, and gimmicks. You're seen as a neighbor, a fellow human being. You can bring back "the human touch" to your message.

Whether you remain with the existing marketing concepts you're using now, or you test-market with some direct response marketing techniques – you must keep swinging. Stay in it for the long haul, and you won't regret it.

Think like your prospect. You may recall the example I used in an earlier chapter about the fisherman who always caught fish when nobody else could. When he shared his strategy with his buddies, he said, "You guys think like a fisherman. I think like the fish."

Always think like your prospects and customers.

When it comes to mindset and connecting with your target market, here's the winning formula:

A. Decide exactly who you want as a customer. Define who they are – their income, net worth, overall affluence, lifestyle and ambitions, aspirations, interests, and attitudes about money.

B. Craft your products and services to match perfectly with your prospects' needs and desires.

C. Go where your ideal prospects are.

The third point is key. It's also the strategy most overlooked by many business owners. Today's consumers, especially affluent consumers, can be best found, identified, effectively communicated with, attracted, and ultimately sold to by using the strategies in this book.

I have done my best to give you the foundation and marketing strategies you need to make your dreams and business a huge success. They have worked for me and for thousands of other small business owners. They will work for you as well.

This is where the information, motivation, and inspiration stops, and the applications of these marketing strategies begin for you.

It's your turn now. You, and you alone, are responsible for taking the action to create the business and lifestyle you've always hoped to have. Nobody else can do it for you.

You can do this, and I think you will do it. Most of all, remember to enjoy the journey.

Ready To Take Your Business To The Next Level...

Specialty Marketing Consultants

Get my monthly "On-Target Marketing" Newsletter FREE at
www.SpecialtyMarketingConsultants.com/newsletter

The **"On Target Marketing"** newsletter is full of practical tips, strategies, and resources to gain more profitably faster. It contains the essential moneymaking strategies to help you *attract*, *convert*, and *keep* your ideal customers, clients, and/or patients.

"Marketing You Can Do Right Now"
(Free Worldwide Podcast)

"Marketing You Can Do Right Now" podcast is free & available on **iTunes** or **Stitcher Radio**. Shows are fast-paced for busy business entrepreneurs and business owners. We cover important can't-miss moneymaking strategies to help you grow your business faster.

"The Copy Wizard"

Are you stuck with your marketing project? Need help understanding the fundamentals of direct response copywriting or writing copy with more personality? This is your resource for the highest level of content creation and direct response copywriting to help you achieve your revenue goals. **www.TheCopyWizard.com**

"Help My Parent Now"

This information product is dedicated to Winnie Townsend, my wonderful 97-year-old mother who has been battling dementia for a few years. In her honor, I've developed *Help My Parent Now,* a concise, comprehensive, compassionate video-based guide for families who are dealing with this devastating disease. For more information, go to: **www.HelpMyParentNow.com** or **www.facebook.com/helpmyparentnow.com**

Getting Your Business Where You Want It To Be

Free Report Example

Revealed Inside This FREE Report:

The 5 Success Secrets Behind The Private, Little-Shared, And Extremely Prosperous World Of ███████ ███████████

The Place Where Successful Executives Gather To Exchange Information And Help Each Other. Welcome To The Most Unique Executive Organization Of Its Kind In America.

Nothing like it occurs <u>anywhere</u> else.

Dear Fellow Executive,

Allow me to begin this letter by asking you: Why have you worked so hard to run your business? You may not have stopped to think about it lately.

It's easy to get caught up in your business – actually working *for* your business, consumed by day-to-day routines, and wind up feeling like the 'Lone Ranger.'

You, running around in circles chased by work, with no navigational compass.

I want to challenge you to re-think why you are in business… a business owner, who bears a responsibility far greater than any employee whose paycheck you sign.

Why Did You REALLY Get Into Business?

… Did you get into business in order to work hard,,. work long hours, every day?

… To fear taking time off?

… To worry about where next week's clients and revenues will come from?

… To provide jobs and pay taxes?

…To work this hard just to pay your bills… or earn a good living?

… "Did You Get Into Business To Be A 'Coal Miner' – Hi Ho… Hi Ho… It's Off To Work I Go?"

Try to remember…

You probably got into business and worked your way to the top so you could have liberty and independence, to be in control, and to enjoy a way above income doing the…

Getting Your Business Where You Want It To Be

Letter Example #1

██████████, *host of 'The* ████████████ *Show," and* ████████████, *CEO of* ██
██████████ – *widely recognized as "Pioneers" in helping private investors – issue one of the*
most important messages of your financial life..."

"Well Known Brokerage Houses And Financial Advisors Treat You Like A Sucker Playing At The Craps Table – But It's Not Just Your Money, It's Your Hopes And Dreams They're Screwing With!"

Worst Of ALL, The Game Has Been Fixed.
They Win. You Lose. Thanks For Playing.

We're Going To Turn The Table On Them And Tell You How They *REALLY* Make Their Money – At Your Expense!

Dear ██████████

Thank you for recently requesting your free report from *Blue Ocean Portfolios*.

We hope you found our report to be a candid insight as to what really goes on in the world of financial investing. **And, if you thought the report was revealing, better hang on to your hat.**

We're About To Break *All* The Rules

We're going to bust through the MYTHS of investing – and give you *more* hardcore truths about what *really* happens when you give your hard-earned money to most brokerage houses and financial advisors.

After reading this letter, you'll be able to tell them to take their ball and go home because…

"…You Won't Have To Play Their Game Anymore"

There's no way to sugarcoat this, so please forgive us for being blunt:

You Are Being Robbed!

Wall Street's "good-old-boy" network is secretly and systematically plundering millions of brokerage accounts. And chances are, yours is one of them.

That's right. And, while urging you to buy their recommended products, brokers and their bosses are quietly collecting huge commission checks – and it's all happening at …

Getting Your Business Where You Want It To Be

Letter Example #2

Congratulations!

You're on the cusp of one of the smartest business decisions you'll ever make for your business.

If you picked up this report hoping for a major breakthrough in your business --- **you've done the right thing** .

I hate to be blunt, but there's no way to sugar coat this...

Most small business advertising and marketing sucks!

Huge sums of money are wasted, and opportunities lost.

Most small businesses are floundering around, uncertain of even the difference between "good" advertising and marketing, and "bad" advertising and marketing.

I realize this is a strong statement, but hang with me here just a second.

The majority of what people know about advertising and marketing doesn't work for small business.

Please don't take this personally.

Actually in fairness to you, it's not really your fault. Over the years, your peers and competitors have set you up for slaughter.

This report is going to clear things up for you, and introduce you to a radical "prescription for change."

... Are you ready?

Okay, for starters...

Newsletter Example #1

Rod Harter's
⊚n Target Marketing

ISSUE #42   *Monthly Newsletter*   FEBRUARY 2016

5 Emotional Marketing Triggers That Determine Why We Buy

When you understand the marketing triggers that make people buy, you can sell more. And you can find more eager customers. Our emotions trigger us to buy. People buy what they want. Needs are driven by logic. Wants are driven by emotions.

We Buy What We Want. Think not? What teenager really needs a cell phone or $200 pair of jeans? Who needs your product? People buy because they want it. Every day we buy things we want instead of things we need.

Don't mistake your market for "everyone who needs your product." You will waste time and money trying to convince people who need your product to want it. The best target market for you is people who **want** your product or service.

Here Are 5 Of Our Strongest Emotions That Control Much Of The Choices We Make.

Love
What do your customers love? It might include their partner, family, pets, business, career, culture, hobbies, books, personal time etc. Do they buy from you for one of these loves? If so, how can you recognize and encourage others with the same love?

Pride
Why does your neighbor buy a bigger screen TV than yours? How did you feel when you first drove home with that new car? Who and what are you proud of? And what would you do to show and protect that pride?

Guilt
Often it might be hard to know the real reason someone bought something new, invested money or gave a gift. Was it love or guilt? I wonder, "Is

People make buying decisions based on EMOTIONS and justify their decisions with LOGIC. Include emotional triggers in your marketing materials.

guilt the real driver behind the spending for Christmas, Valentines and Mothers' Day?"

Can the guilt of not buying motivate your prospect into buying? Can you use guilt to up sell?

Fear
This may be our most powerful driver. It is likely this emotion, more than any other, has helped humanity to survive.

What fear might motivate your prospect to buy from you? Will not buying expose them to risk, missed opportunities or embarrassment? Many professional buyers operate on the fear principle.

They fear the consequence of making the wrong decision. How can you use or diminish that fear to make them buy from you? Why is it that people who know they need to get fit suddenly change their diet and start exercising after their first heart attack? The fear of dying makes them want to be fit.

Greed
— "Greed is Good." according to Gordon Gecko in

Newsletter Example #2

On Target Marketing
Rod Harter's
Monthly Newsletter

| ISSUE #34 | | APRIL 2015 |

Having Trouble Getting Your Message Across? Then, Think Of Your "Marketing" As "Flirting"...

Do You Hit The Panic Button When You Think Of The Word "Marketing?"

If so, you're not alone. Many people feel the same about marketing as they do public speaking. They hate it. They'd rather spend an afternoon in the dental chair than take on the riggers of a marketing campaign. *Have you ever found yourself...*

- ✓ Not knowing **where to start** a marketing project...
- ✓ Not knowing how to **"write with personality"** when you communicate with **prospects and clients...**
- ✓ Not knowing how to **tie everything together** in a natural, sequential order...

If you've followed us for any time at all, you know we like to make complicated things "simple". **For many, marketing is a major roadblock.** If that applies to you, consider the following... when marketing, try replacing the word marketing with the word "storytelling." Great marketing is nothing more than your ability to tell your story.

Instead of stopping there, let's take things a step further. As you tell your stories...

Have Some Fun. Start "Flirting" A Little With Your Audience

We *all* know how to flirt. Flirting is basically a playful game we have with others we want to be attracted to us... **and ultimately choose us.**

Start flirting with your prospects and clients (in a business way).

Neither Marketing Or Flirting Have A Fixed Set Of Rules... Per Say

Flirting, is usually playful, bordering on silly sometimes. We flirt best when we don't take things too seriously. We create an element that's carefree. That's not to say you can throw caution to the wind. **Always remain a pro.** Be smart about it. Tell your story. In the process, invite your prospects and clients into your world.

When you think of marketing this way, you'll remove some of the mental barriers. In time, the process will get easier. Of course, always keep things professional. **Relax, and be yourself.** When you do, your prospects and clients will find you to be more personable and attractive.

When your audience finds you attractive... watch out! **You'll soon be attracting all the clients, customer, or patients you'll ever want!**

BE INSPIRED.
CHANGE YOUR BUSINESS.

Are you ready for immediate, massively experienced, and personalized help to solve everything that's holding up profits or keeping your business from moving to the next level?

Sometimes, the best way to start is with a phone call.

We can have a private one-on-one, conversation together, and know quickly if my company is your best choice for your project. We'll figure out what you need, and the fee to make it happen.

If you're serious about getting the best possible insights and advice from a respected, proven copywriter and direct-marketing professional, let me hear from you.

You can reach me two ways.

Phone: (407) 619-3598
Email: RodHarter@me.com

58109147R00075